Amazing Mosaic Garden

Surprising Designs in Various Techniques

Sigalit Eshet

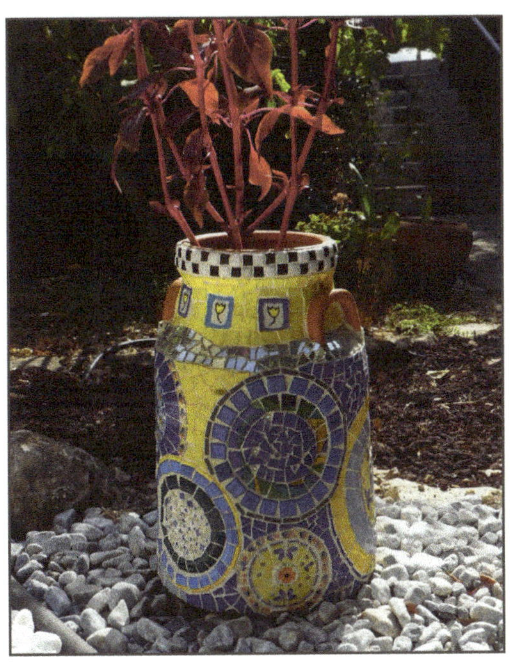

First Print Edition: 2022

Photographs by Efrat Tenenbaum and Sigalit Eshet

Translation: Michaeli Translations

ISBN: 978-965-92827-6-0

www.sigalit.art

Disclaimer

All do-it-yourself activities involve risk, and your safety is your own responsibility, including proper use of equipment and safety gear, and determining whether you have adequate skill and experience.

Some of the resources used for these projects are dangerous unless used properly and with adequate pre-cautions, including safety gear.

Some illustrative photos do not depict safety precautions or equipment, in order to show the project step more clearly.

Some projects are user-submitted, and appearance of a project in this format does not indicate it has been checked for safety or functionality. Use of the instructions and suggestions is at your own risk.

I disclaim all responsibility for any resulting damage, injury, or expense. It is your responsibility to make sure that your activities comply with all applicable laws.

Contents

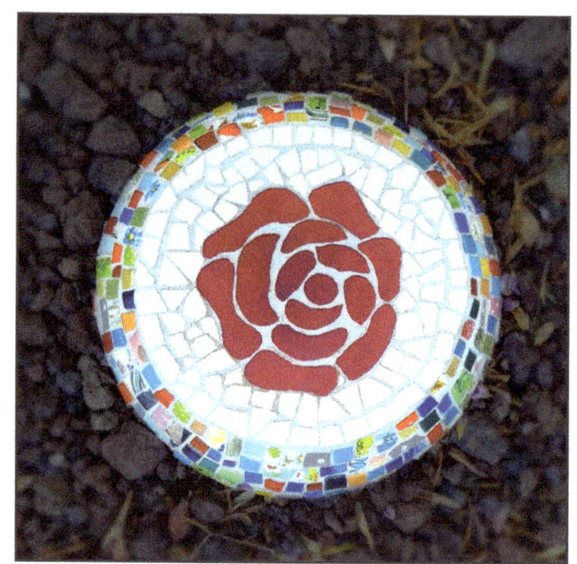

Introduction

The art of mosaic is varied and rich, allowing to transform any surface into mosaic art. Originally, mosaic is a very ancient art that began centuries before Christ, by putting together chiseled rocks. It was first used to decorate floors and later even walls. Additional techniques evolved, and materials were added in time, from cut up stones to shiny glass. Nowadays, you can make mosaic from a wide range of materials and make practical as well as decorative products, small items in micro-mosaic, and giant walls.

This book will focus on mosaic pieces that fit home and gardens, that can decorate your garden or porch for many years: plant pots, spheres, steppingstones, tables, two-dimensional mosaic as well as three-dimensional ones.

True, it might sometimes seem hard, and perhaps there are projects that might look complicated to you at first, but if you follow them step-by-step, you'll see that you can also create them yourselves; and with time and practice gained, you can also invent your own designs and enjoy making them. My goal is to give you ideas which you could then copy, using the samples attached to the book, or simply let your imagination soar, following a new technique you've learned.

My name is Sigalit, a mosaic artist, manufacturer, and teacher.

I've been involved in mosaics for many years. I fell in love with this art for its colorfulness, variety of materials, myriad of techniques and the opportunity to innovate, invent, design and work both creatively and technically. I find myself learning from each project and student and enjoy finding those small "tips" that help in the process of mosaic making, while creating new designs, which I gladly share with my students and readers.

In this book I collected many examples of mosaics that fit any garden. You can obviously keep these works indoor, but I've decided to focus on works that can be placed outside without worrying about ruining the mosaic. Here you will have many ideas for such works, as well as photographed projects that will take you step-by-step on your way to making a mesmerizing mosaic piece. The finished products can decorate any garden or porch and add color and joy.

This is the ninth book in the series, and I hope you enjoy it just as you have enjoyed the previous ones and get new ideas for your next mosaic work.

On page 83 you'll find a link to a file containing all examples – have fun!

I guarantee you a colorful and joyful experience!

Sigalit

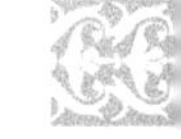

Mosaic Cutting Tools

There are various tools used for mosaic work, and it's recommended that you have at least the basic ones in your arsenal. Each material will have its own best-suited tool. Using the right tool can make the work tremendously easier and more accurate.

Since this book covers the use of various materials, I recommend that you own at least one of each tool shown here (at least for cutting glass and ceramics). Naturally, you can choose whichever material you desire for making the suggested examples.

Below are detailed instructions on working with each instrument.

Ceramic Cutting

Mosaic Tile Cutter (1) – For cutting and grinding ceramic tiles. You can get these in hardware stores.

Compound Tile Nipper (2) – For cutting and grinding ceramic tiles. This tool has twice the power of a conventional cutter. You can find it online or in specialized stores. I love using this tool, as it's strong and easy to cut with.

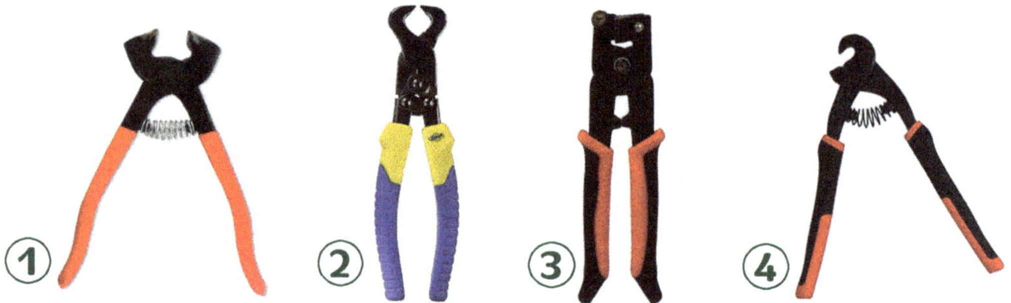

Combined Tile Cutting Clamp (3) – A technique taken from glass sheet cutting. Using the clamp, you first make notches in the tile and then cut it. A simple replacement to a cutting machine or curved cuts.

Parrot Beak Nipper (4) – Intended for making dents in tiles, when you want to make curved and dented shapes, such as hearts or rose petal. See detailed explanation on how to use this nipper on the rose table project.

Ceramic Cutting Machine – For advanced cutters. Used to cut ceramic into straight and accurate tiles. I did not use this cutting machine for any projects in this book.

Hammer – For cutting thick ceramic, or when you want to cut random shapes. Please note that when you cut ceramic with a hammer, you should wrap the ceramic with an old towel and place it on top of a thick wood or metal surface.

Glass Cutting Tools

Wheeled Glass Nipper – For cutting glass and plates.

For cutting any kind of glass – surfaces or squares – as well as cutting plates and cups. Can be found in stores that sell glass cutting equipment.

If you wish to integrate glass from a large panel into the mosaic, you'll need several other tools used for cutting glass (also used for making stained glass). I like using these panels for their shine and pleasing appearance, and since they come in a wide variety of colors. There are also places that sell pre-cut glass stripes of glass, which can sometimes make it easier on cutting.

Glass Cutter – For cutting straight lines or specific shapes. There are several kinds of cutters. The difference is in shape and price. I recommend you to try out and decide which cutter works best for you. All cutters have a small wheel at the top, and the difference is mainly in the grip angle.

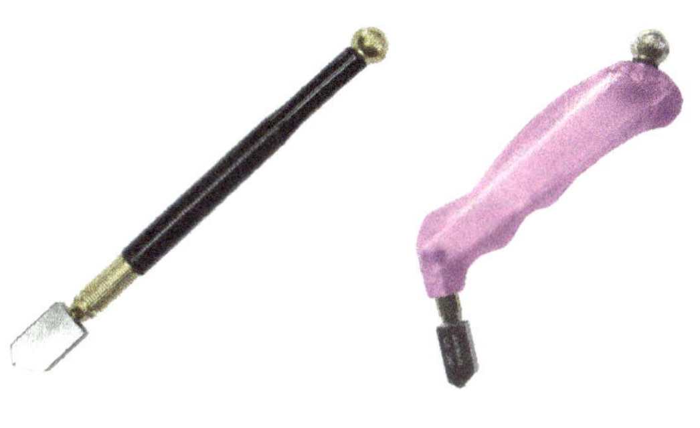

Pliers

Breaking glass plier/Running plier – For Breaking glass after marking it with the glass cutter.

Grozer pliers - For breaking glass along score lines that can't be handled comfortably by hand. The cutter has two sides, one straight and the one curved.

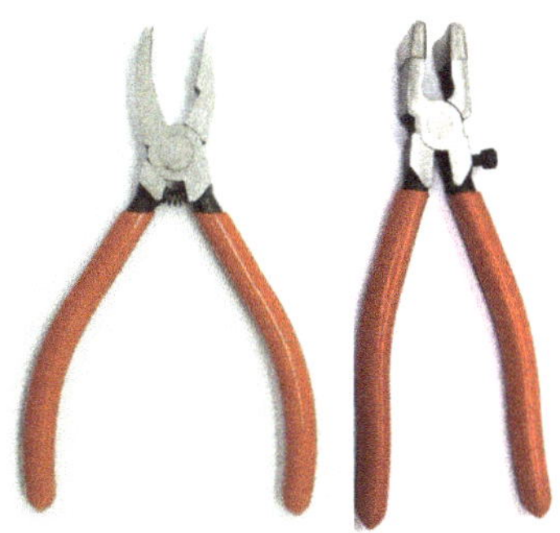

Mosaic Equipment and Preparation Tools

The additional mosaic making tools are not expensive and can easily be attained:

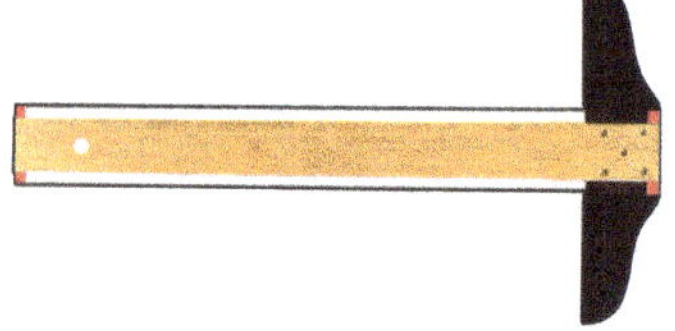

Pencil – For drawing the desired pattern on the substrate material.

Ruler – For marking straight lines.

T-Ruler – For guiding the glass cut into straight lines.

Tweezers – For placing small pieces.

Glass Paint Marker – For marking shapes on the glass. It's better to have one black and one white or gold, for dark glass panels.

Latex Gloves – For protecting your hands against scratches and dirt.

Rubber Gloves – Put these on before you start working with grout.

Plastic Containers – For glue, water, cut glass or beads and mixing colors.

Small Brush – For cleaning the surface from dust and small particles.

Thin Flat Screwdriver – For cleaning tile adhesive residue.

Paintbrush – For adhesive application.

Wooden Mixing Sticks – For mixing grout and applying tile adhesive.

Carbon Paper – To copy your design from paper onto your substrate material.

Spatula – For applying tile adhesive. This tool is usually used by painters but is very efficient in applying tile adhesive.

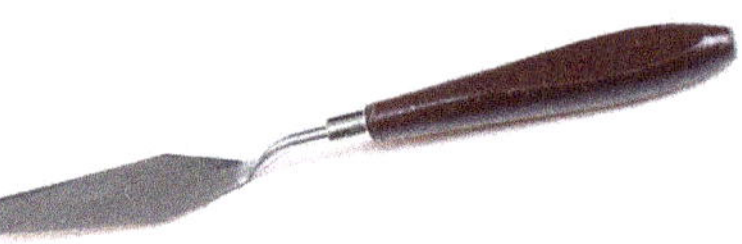

Safety Equipment

Safety goggles – For protecting your eyes against ceramic fragments. Use it when cutting ceramic.

Dust mask – Use this when preparing the grout.

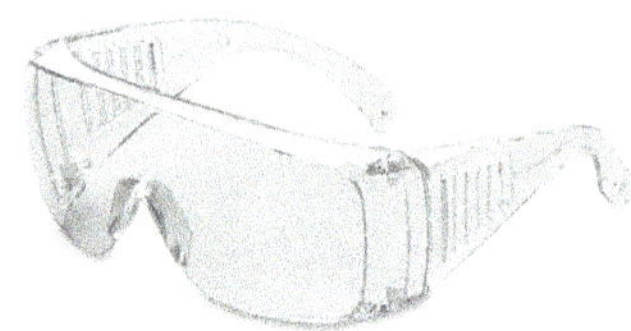

Safety Instructions

Safety is imperative when making mosaic. Glass and cut ceramic have sharp edges and can shoot out toward you, so use caution.

1. Always wear closed shoes. Don't walk barefoot on the floor where you are working. Small fragments can be difficult to spot and remove.
2. Wear safety goggles and gloves when cutting glass plates.
3. Use a small brush to clean the working surface. Don't clean the small fragments with your bare hands!
4. Vacuum the floor after finishing – it's better than just sweeping dust around.
5. Keep young children and pets away.
6. Keep some adhesive bandages at hand.

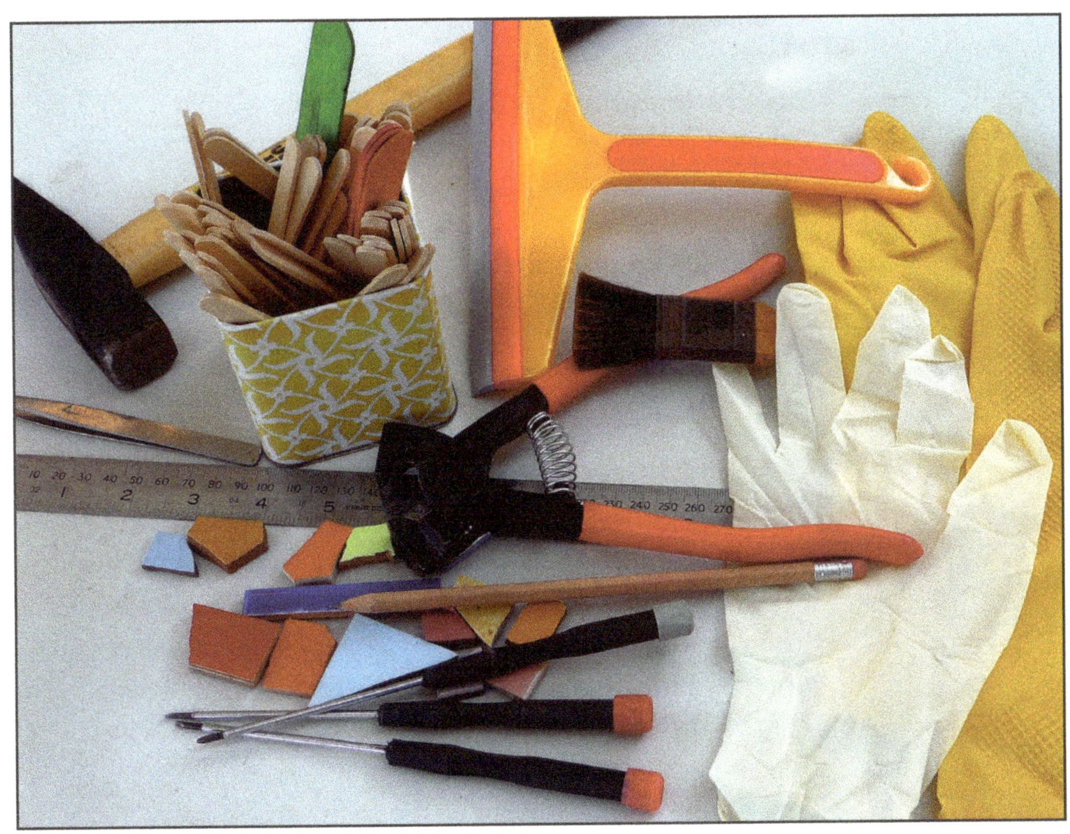

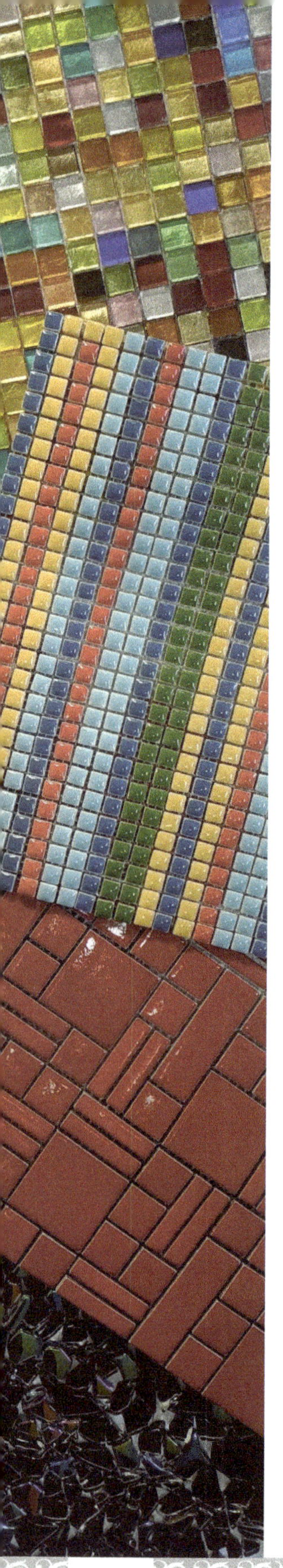

Materials

The list of materials to be used in a mosaic work can be very long, and that is what I love so much about it – you can and should combine different types of materials, depending on the work of course. There are gentler materials that are only suitable for works that stay indoors and other that will last outdoors for many years.
In this book you will find versatile works that incorporate different materials. I suggest you experiment and choose the materials you'd like to work with for yourselves. In works that remain outdoors, you should avoid using plastic pieces that might fade in the sunlight or peel off.
The following list details materials that are suitable for mosaic work, but you can of course try and incorporate any materials you see fit, or anything else interesting you might find.

Colorful Ceramic Tiles – Can be found in a variety of shapes and sizes.

Glass Tiles – These come in uniform size squares and in many colors. They have one smooth, flat side (which should face up), and a rough side (to which glue is applied).

Stained Glass – Can be found in many colors and textures. You can cut it with a nipper or a glass cutter.

Ceramic Square Tiles – These are available in many colors, textures, and shapes. They come mostly on a square mesh.

Vitreous Glass Mosaic Tiles – Ready-made square glass tiles in a variety of sizes and colors. The glass can be glossy or grainy, clear or opaque, uniform or blended. Tile sizes start at 1 cm^2/0.15in^2, and you can buy them by sheets of sticker tiles or by weight.

China and Crockery – Using the proper safety precautions, these can be broken or used to cut your own tiles. Plates often have that unique texture that you can't find in tiles.

Found Objects – These include seashells, glass beads, buttons, glass nuggets, necklaces, brooches, etc. Use it to decorate and enrich your work.

Mirrors – These can add a beautiful reflective touch to any mosaic piece.

Polymer clay – Use polymer clay, like Fimo™, to decorate your mosaic work.

Beads – I like incorporating different types of beads into mosaics: glass or plastic, round or square, tiny or large. Each necklace that falls out of my favor ends up in my bead box, and quickly finds its way into a mosaic piece.

Smalti – Colored glass chunks with very vivid colors. We'll leave the smalti for more advanced installments; the book will not cover this material.

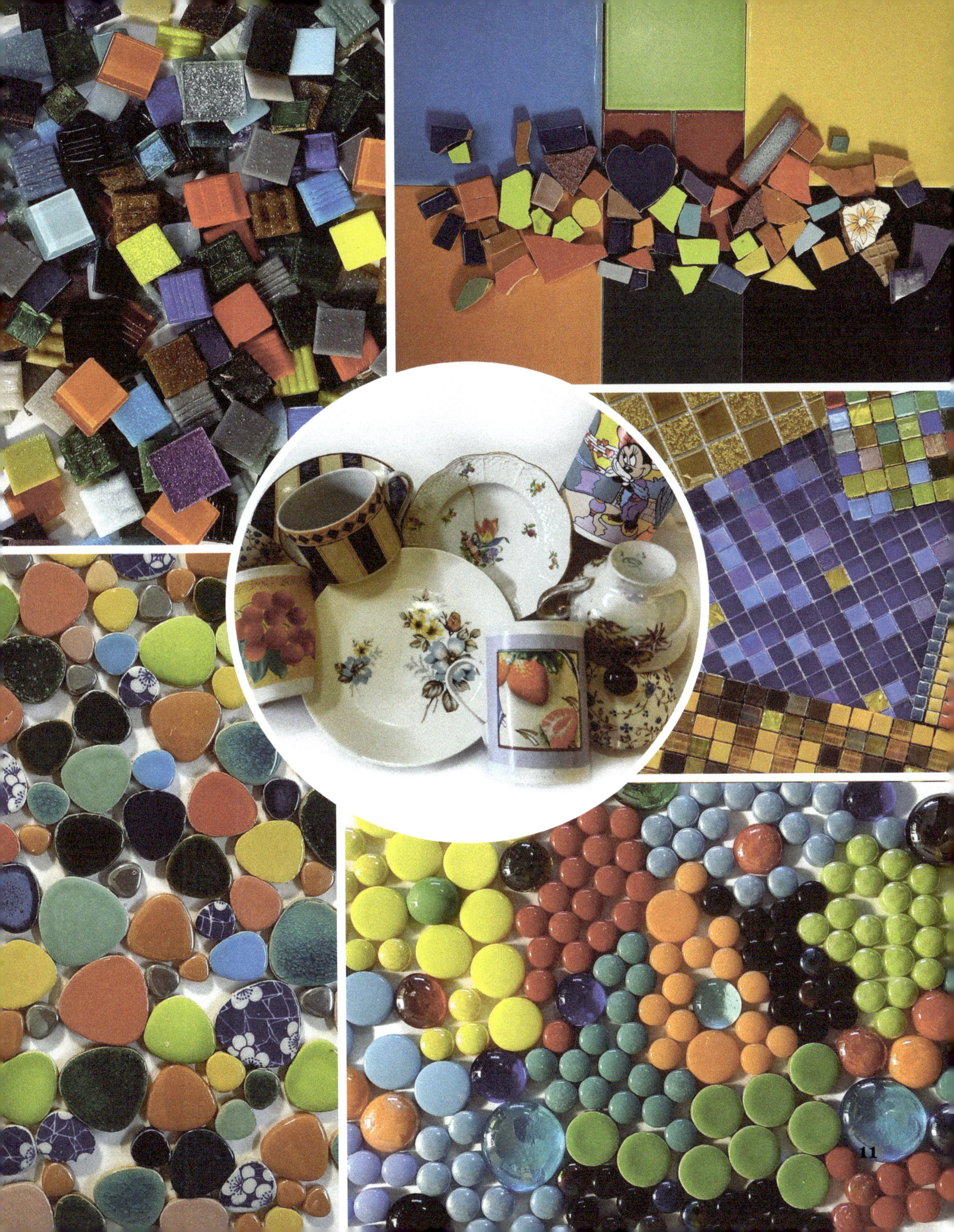

Adhesives

Remember! It's important to use adhesives correctly. You should always read the manufacture instructions. I recommend using the adhesive that's most comfortable for you.

It's very important to match the adhesive to the piece's base material. For instance, when you glue on a wood surface, only use white plastic glue. This glue suits mosaic works that won't come in contact with wetness, dampness or direct sunlight; meaning, pieces that will be stored in a safe place or would be used as a temporary adhesive for gluing on meshes.

In case the piece's base is metal, concrete or ceramics, or in case we've chosen to create a mosaic that will remain outdoors, you should use tile adhesive – this way, the piece will have no problem staying outside, at any weather.

There are many types of adhesives. I'll detail the ones we'll use in this book:

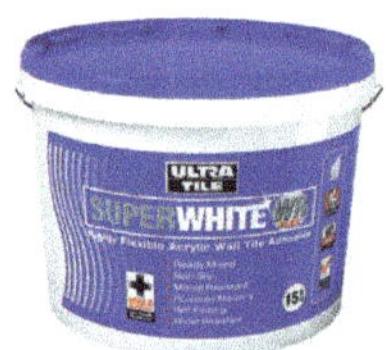

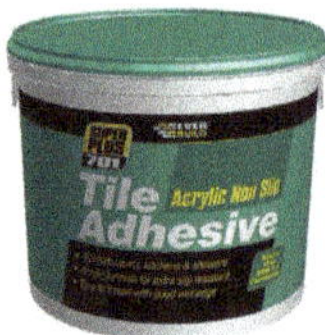

Tile Glue – Used to glue ceramic tiles on metal, clay or any other surface that is meant for the outdoors, to be exposed the elements. This glue comes in a form of powder that needs to be mixed with water (make as much as you need each time) or in a ready-made box. Once it settles, the glue becomes stone hard, that is why you must work with a small batch every time.

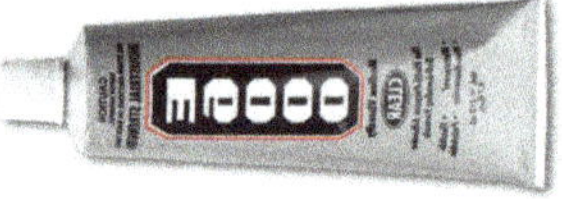

Glass Glue – For sticking tiles onto a glass substrate (like E6000).

Silicone Glue – Comes in a tube and is for gluing relatively small surfaces. Useful for gluing wall tiles when you are looking for quick and strong gluing. You should choose a gluing adhesive and not a sealing one (like Super 7).

Plastic or Carpenter's Glue – Used as a temporary adhesive for gluing on a mesh, before gluing the work onto the surface using tile adhesive.

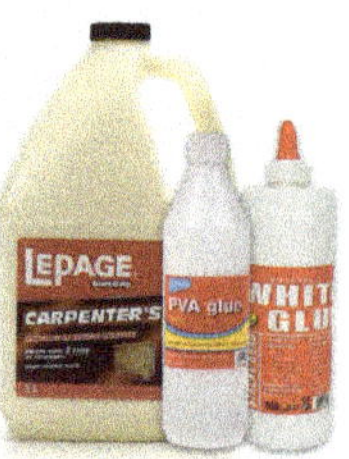

Grout

Grout is a colorful powder mixed with water and used to fill the gaps between the tiles – usually floor and wall tiles. In mosaic work, grout is used as a finisher, to fill the gaps between the cut tiles. In addition, it reinforces the work and brings all the pieces together for one complete work. The grout also levels the height differences between the cut tiles and smoothens the mosaic. Later, we'll see several situations in which the grout can be expanded as a finisher.

The grout comes in different colors matching your project. White grout can be versified using acrylic paint or color pigments, as long as the final work is not exposed to sun or water. It's important to mix the grout itself according to the manufacture instructions.

Working with grout might get messy, so it's important to wear the right clothes, cover the surface with a newspaper and put on gloves. You should make time out of your day to apply the grout since you cannot stop in the middle – the grout will harden and will be very hard to clean.

Before applying the grout, make sure the following is ready:

A Plastic Container – For making the grout.

Wooden Stirring Sticks – For mixing the grout.

Latex Gloves – For protecting your hands.

A Small Plastic Wiper or Spatula (a silicone spatula for cream) – For picking up and applying the grout on even surfaces.

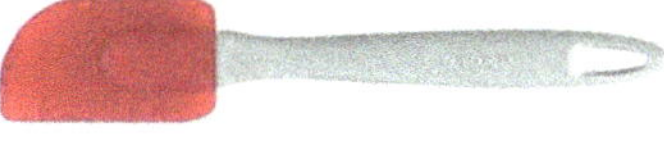

Sponge or Cotton Rags – For grout cleaning.

Old Newspapers – For placing under your work to maintain a clean surface.

Water – For preparing grout and cleaning.

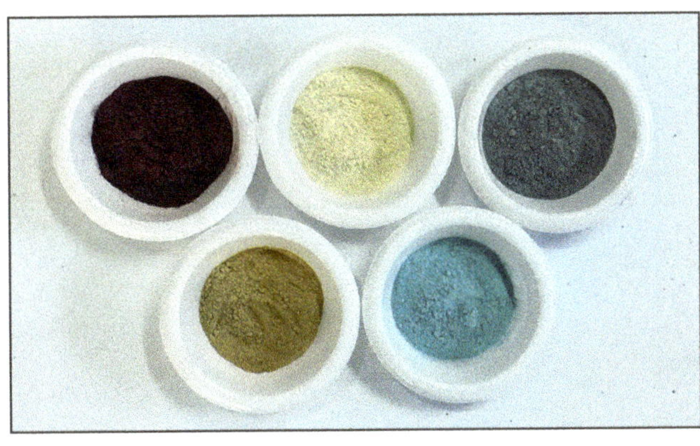

Choosing the Right Grout Color

The color of grout you select will significantly influence the final look. In fact, if you create the exact same piece twice with different grout finishes, the mosaic will look utterly different.

When choosing the grout color, ask yourselves what you want to emphasize – the shape or the background? Perhaps the harmony of the mosaic?

A few tips to help you choose the most appropriate color:

1. If your mosaic has a main subject and a background, make sure the background blends in and doesn't contest the subject. Figure out which color can highlight the main image, should it be light or dark, and what will its effect on the subject be.
2. If you're not sure about the right color of grout – gray seems to always get the job done. It's a neutral color suitable for most pieces. Remember that the final work will have a lighter shade than when it's wet during processing.
3. Pieces with colored glass should be complemented with dark grout, as it emphasizes and intensifies the glass' colors.
4. Sometimes it's best to treat grout as an additional color in the work, which gives it more depth. Here, you should use colored grout that will blend in with the mosaic without taking over.
5. Try to avoid using white grout – it highlights blemishes in the work. Use it when you wish to accentuate a white look or when the mosaic is glued tightly on a white background.
6. You can pour a little grout powder into the crack between the tesserae in one of the piece's corners to test and see which color you get.
7. Sometimes, when working with tile glue, it's hard to clean up after and parts of the adhesive fill up the gaps between the tiles. In this case, grout in the same color as the adhesive (usually cream-colored) would be a good fit.

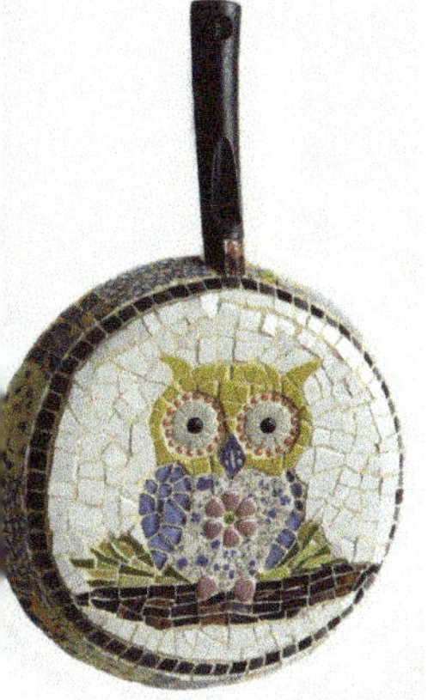

Project: Owl on an Upside-Down Pan

Before throwing away any cooking appliances in my house I first check if they're good for mosaicking – as a surface or even material.

A metal pan that was replaced with a new one is a great surface for a mosaic and a great decoration for the outer house walls. It already comes with a hook and hole; it has a flat and smooth base and there's a nice round extension around that fits the frame. Absolutely perfect! And as long as you are hanging the pan outdoors, it should have a nice owl on it as well.

This work has many materials, each has its own role and place: shards of ceramics, cups and plates, beads, glasses, ready-made squares – everything coming together for a happy image.

Materials:

A metal pan
Colorful kitchenware shards
Orange semi-circles for the eyes
Black glass nuggets for the pupils
White ceramic tiles for the background
Brown glass for the tree trunk
Black and grey squares for the frame
Wheeled glass nipper
Tile cutter
Tile adhesive
Glue container
A wooden spoon or spatula
Light yellow colored grout
Grout Gear: mixing bowl, water, a wooden stick, rags, gloves

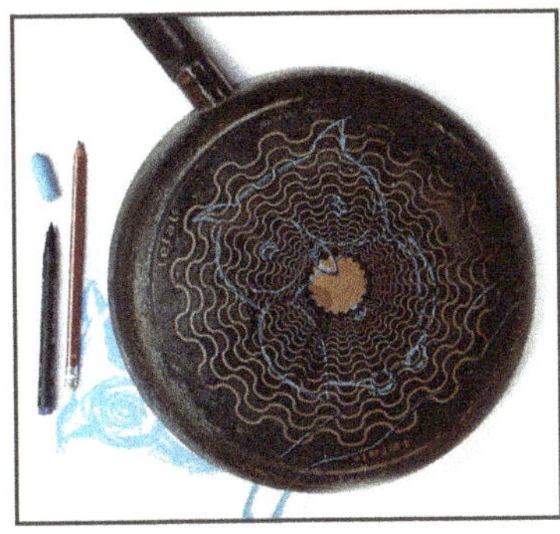

1 Trace the owl onto the pan.
In case the pan is black, we cannot use a tracing paper, so you can do it in the following way:
- Cut the circle with the owl drawing.
- Flip the paper with the pattern to the other side.
- Paint the outline of the drawing using a strong crayon. This will serve as a replacement for the tracing paper.
- Flip the paper back and position it on the upside-down pan. It's recommended to tape the edges, so the paper won't move.
- Using a pencil, press down on the outline to copy the sample onto the surface.

2 Start the owl from gluing the eyes: first, a round black glass nugget at the center, surrounded by snub-nosed white triangles, surrounded in turn, with small orange circles. Glue everything down using tile glue.

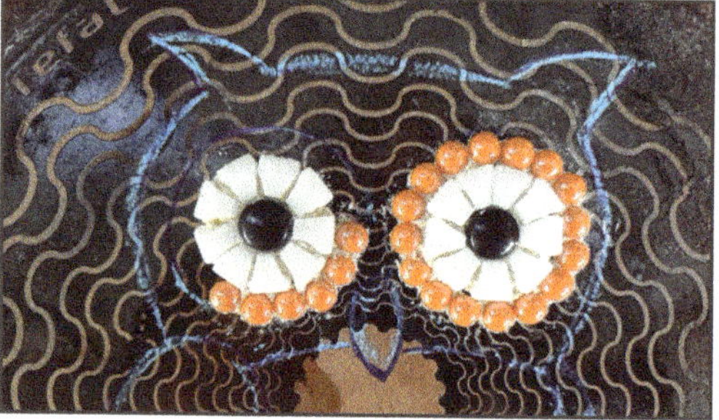

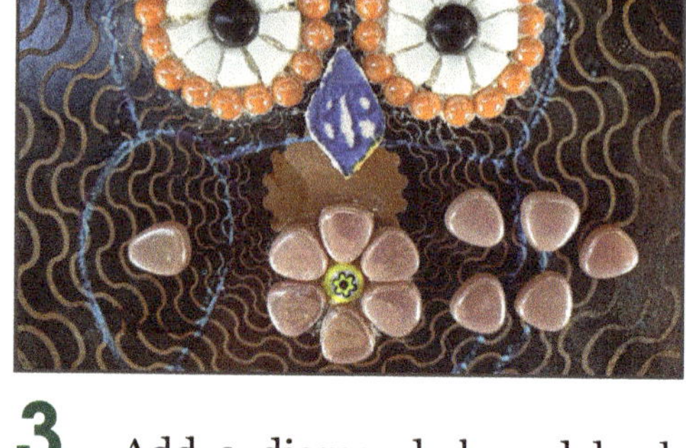

3 Add a diamond-shaped beak (can be cut from a colorful plate) and a flower. I used ready-made, tear-shaped pieces here.

4 The wings of the owl are made of blue mosaic pieces. I've used ready-made pieces in various shapes. One wing is full and the other only outlined.

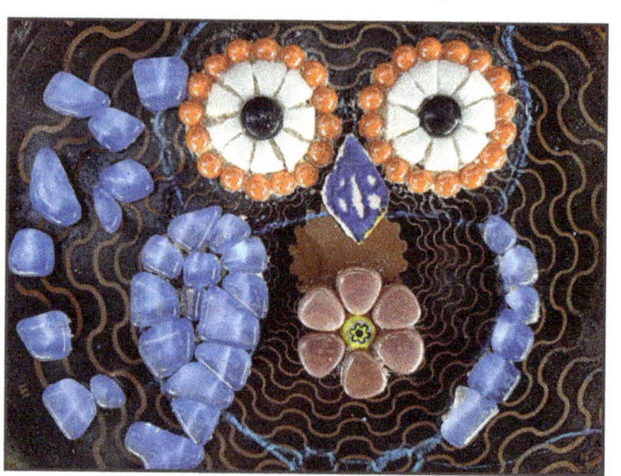

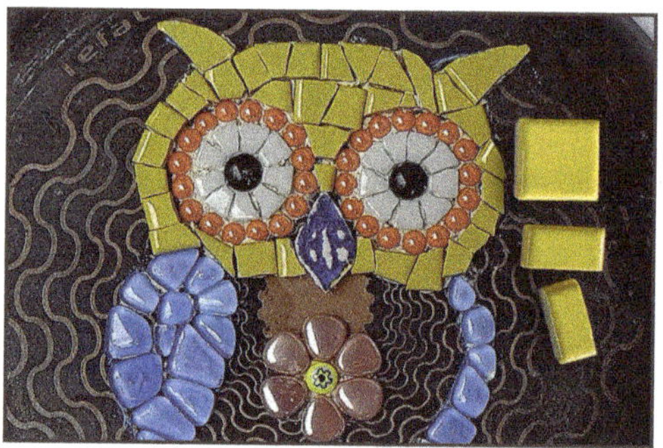

5 Fill in the face of the owl in yellow. Cut yellow ceramics into tiny pieces and glue them. It's important to cut the ears from one nice piece. You can paint the shape on a tile and cut a curved triangle.

6 The belly of the owl is made of shards from a colorful mug. Using the wheeled nipper, cut the mug into small pieces (see a separate explanation on kitchenware cutting).

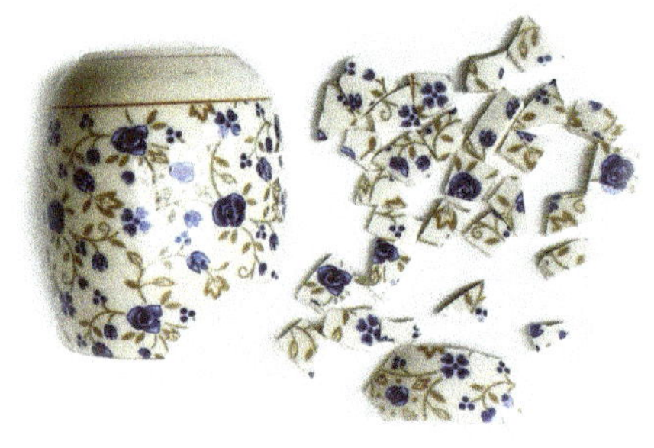

7 Glue two legs to the owl and complete the belly with the cutout mug pieces. Make sure to glue them close together.

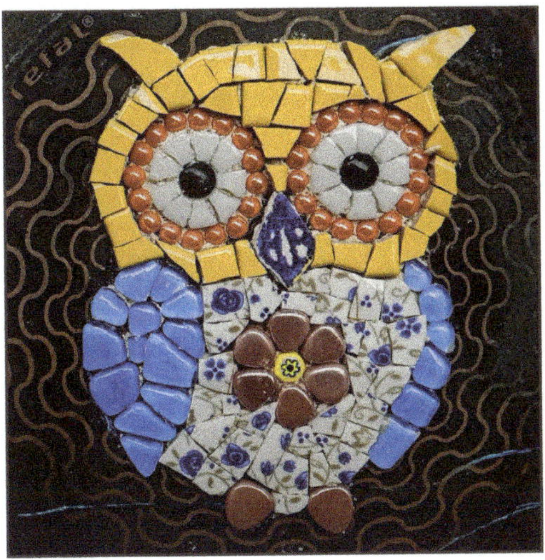

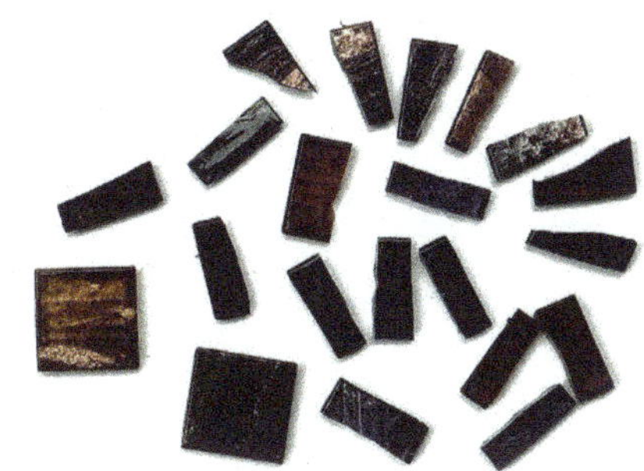

8 The branch is made of brown glass. To add some shine to it, I used glass squares with a copper stripe. Using the wheeled nipper, cut the squares into little stripes – two or three stripes each.

9 Glue the branch under the owl, add stripes in green shades above it, cut the same way.

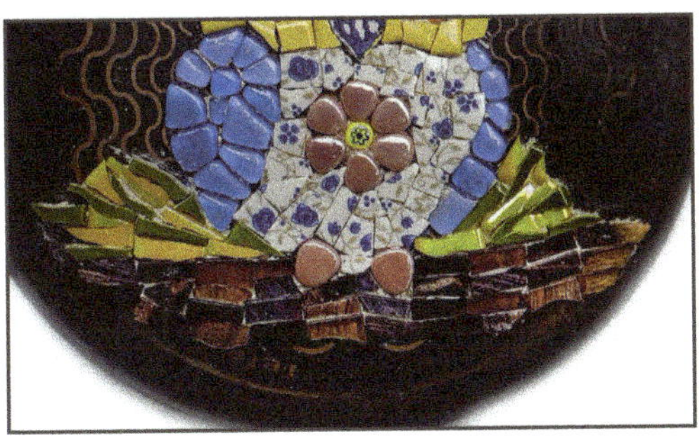

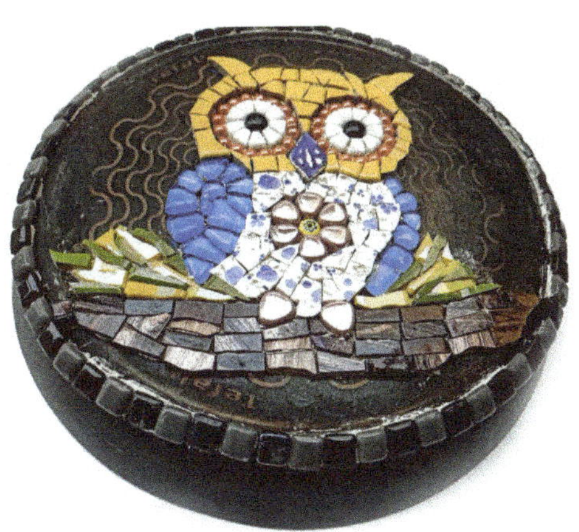

10 Before you prepare the background, it's time to frame it with black and grey squares. Glue them on and make sure it's straight.

11 Cut white ceramics to little pieces using the tile cutter and fill up the background, closely knit.

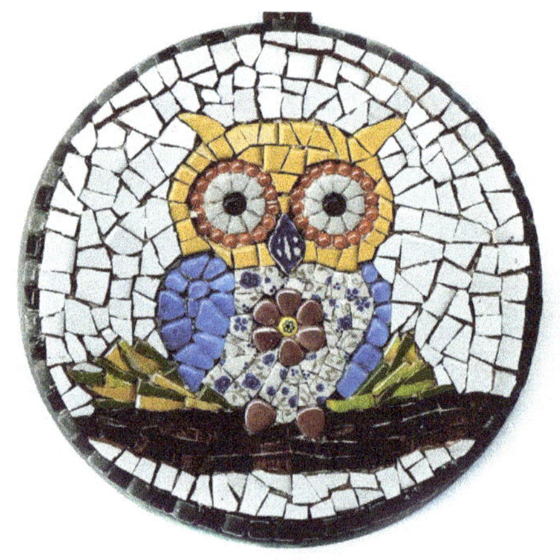

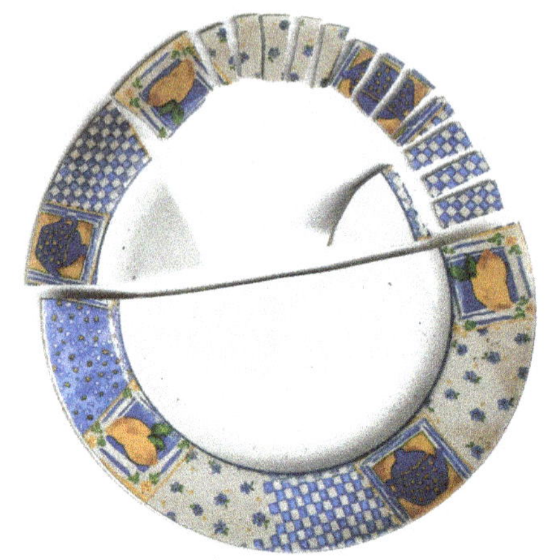

12 Cut a colorful plate frame in two using the nipper. Keep cutting until you get thin and colorful stripes. (See plate cutting instructions on page 35).

13 Cut the stripes to squares and glue them around the edges of the pan. You can make patterns according to the plate you find. Wait a day until it dries well and make the yellow grout.

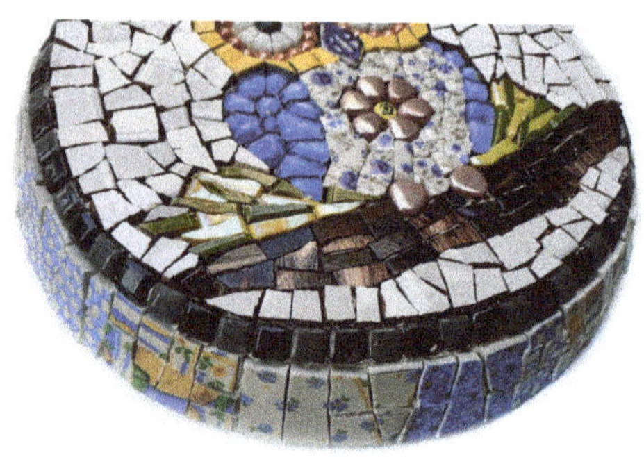

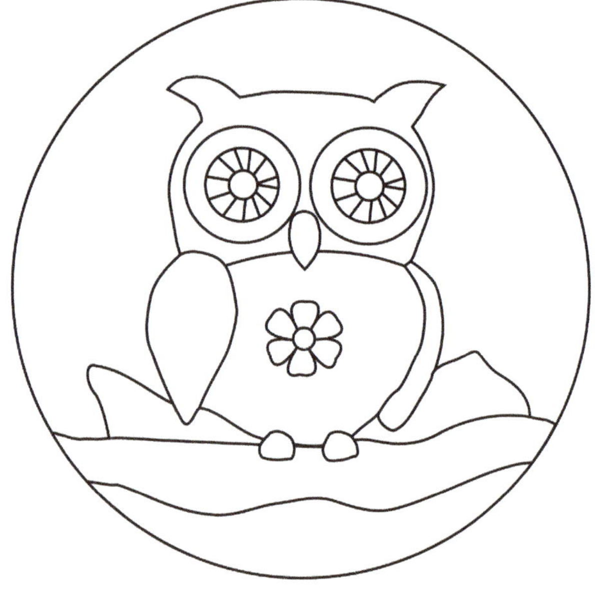

Pattern for the Owl:
Enlarge on a photocopier according to the pan size.

Tip: Filling surfaces with a unified colored ceramic. You can apply glue on the entire surface and fill it in with precut tiles or the other way around: take a piece of ceramics, find its right place, then apply glue on it and paste it.

Applying a grout - step by step:

1 Wear a dust mask to protect your face and wear gloves on your hands.

2 Cover the work surface with old newspapers.

3 Add a few teaspoons of grout in the right color (light yellow, in this case) to a plastic bowl or a disposable container.

4 Pour some water on the grout bowl. Mix with a wooden stick until it cream-like in texture. Notice the manufacture instructions to reach best results.

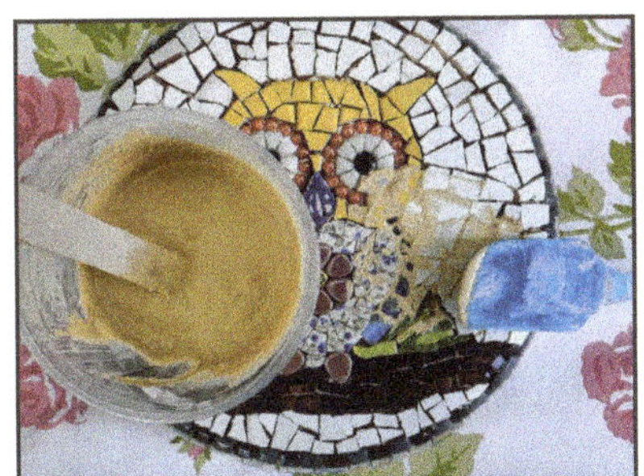

5 Start applying: Pour some grout on the pan. Using a pastry spatula, apply the grout until it fills in all the grooves and holes. Make sure to fill in with grout in the sides as well.

6 Once the piece is covered with grout, use the side of the spatula to scoop and remove the excess.

7 A few minutes later, when it starts to settle, start cleaning: Dampen the piece using a clean cotton rag or a sponge. Use a wet (squeezed) and dry rag several times until the piece is clean. Make sure to occasionally replace the water.
It's important to make sure **to keep the grout wet**. This causes the grout to slowly dry out and prevents cracks. You shouldn't skip this step!

8 If you find "holes" after the cleaning process, fill with grout, let it dry and clean until you get a smooth and clean mosaic.

9 Adhesive residue can be cleaned with wooden skewer or a thin screwdriver.

10 At the end of the work you can be polish it with a wet wipe.

11 If some tile falls during grouting, clean the place well. Wait until the end of grouting process and then glue the fallen part (you can use speed glue), wait for completely drying and fill the holes with grout.

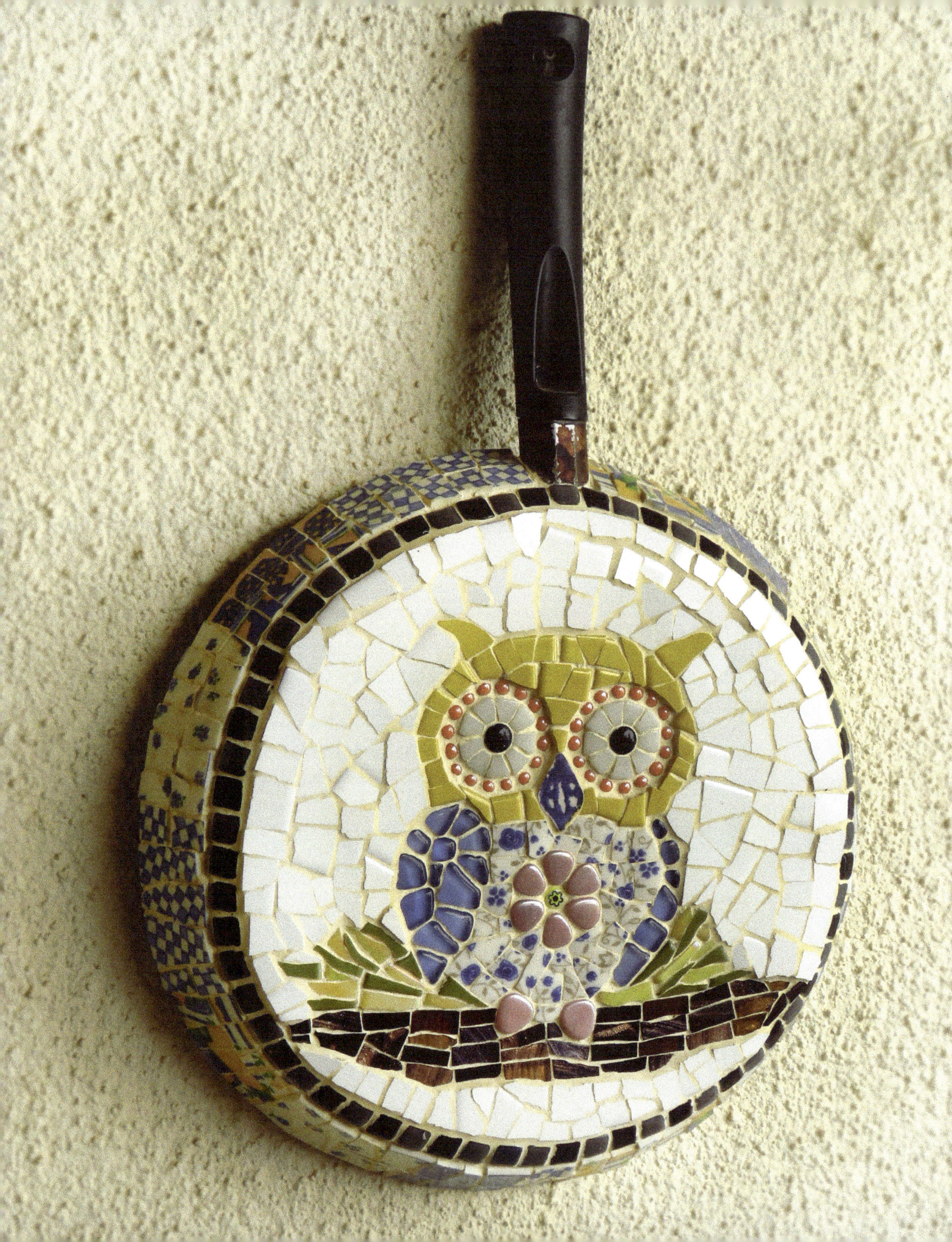

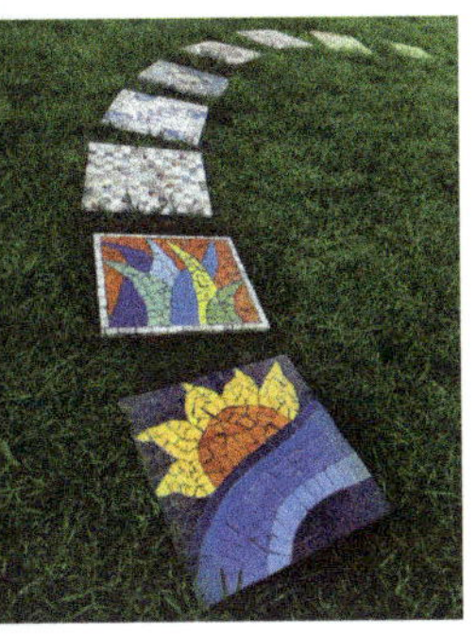

Project: Steppingstones

If you have a garden or entryway, why not decorate it with steppingstones you've prepared yourself? It's in fact a picture mounted on a tile, which means there is an unlimited number of options and designs. You can create a path from similar stones, to create a pattern, or versify and make each one look completely different to get a colorful pathway.
I live in a small village, and every house has its own garden. Since I've designed my pathway, the steppingstones have become extremely popular with my students… in addition, we've prepared a communal project of steppingstones where families prepared such tiles – each according to their own imagination and ability – and the colorful tiles decorate the town's playground paths.
Bellow are three examples of steppingstones, each from a different direction, so you can get a few ideas.

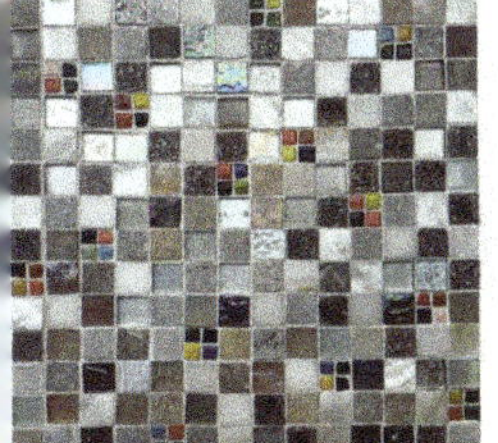

Tile no.1

A steppingstone made of ready-made squares – a natural stone and shiny, brown-hued gems, combined with small colorful squares.
The idea in this example is that each line is made of pretty much the same hues, but different locations. A sort of a systematic chaos. Each line has a spot with 4 small colorful squares.
To make this happen I've made a layout of the positioning of the small squares. You can mix all the rest.

Materials:

Thick ceramic tile measuring 30x30 cm/11.8x11.8"
Natural stone squares and shiny, natural, and brown hued gems, measuring 2x2 cm/0.78"x0.78"
Small colorful squares measuring 0.5x0.5 cm / 0.2x0.2"
Tile glue
A wooden stick or spatula for applying the glue
A thick screwdriver or toothpick to clean excess glue
Small glue bowl
Cream-colored grout
Grout Gear: Mixing bowl, water, a wooden stick, rags, gloves

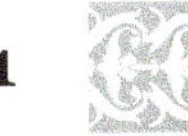

1 Prepare the tile and all stones on a workstation, next to the layout that will help us easily place the stones in each row.

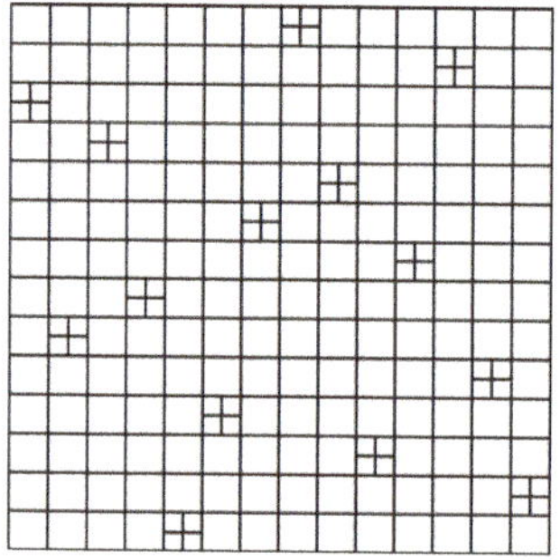

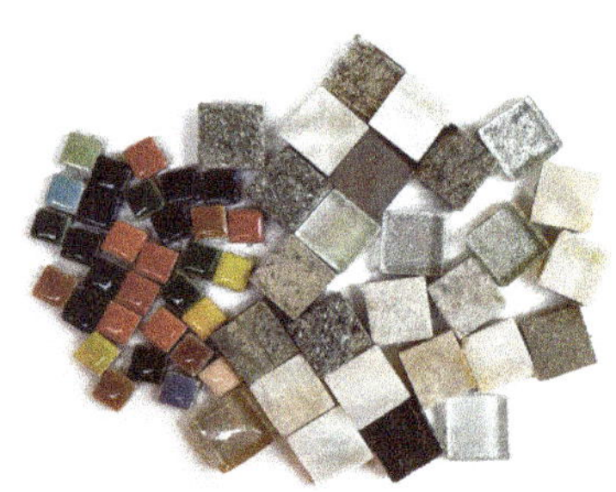

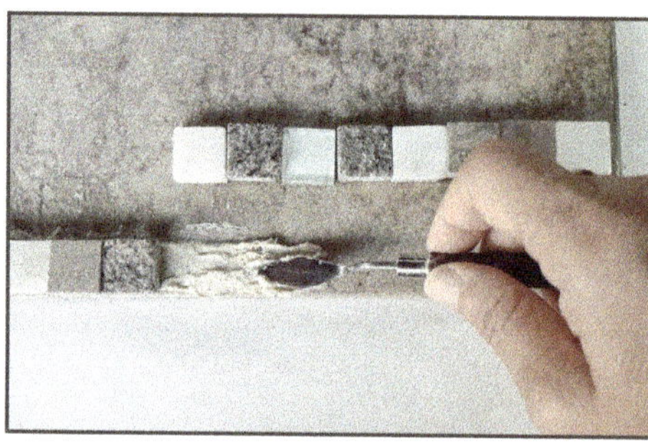

2 Start from the first row: It's recommended to apply the glue tile glue on the entire row, using the spatula, and place the squares on it. Alternatively, you can apply glue on each square and place it on the tile.

3 Continue this way until the tile is full. To make sure the lines are straight, especially aligning the stones at the edge of the tiles for a straight frame, place the tile to dry at least one day before preparing the grout.

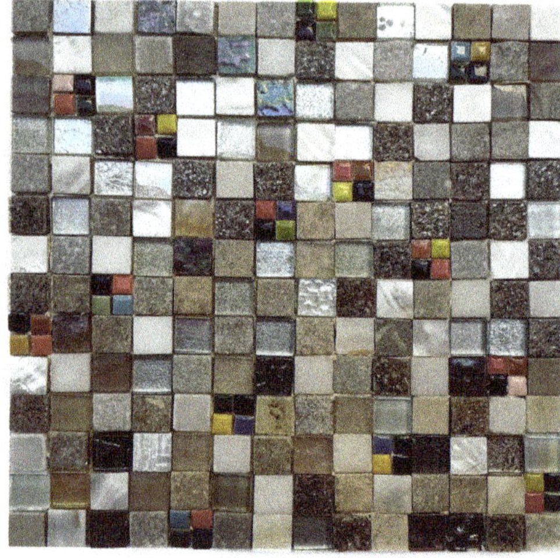

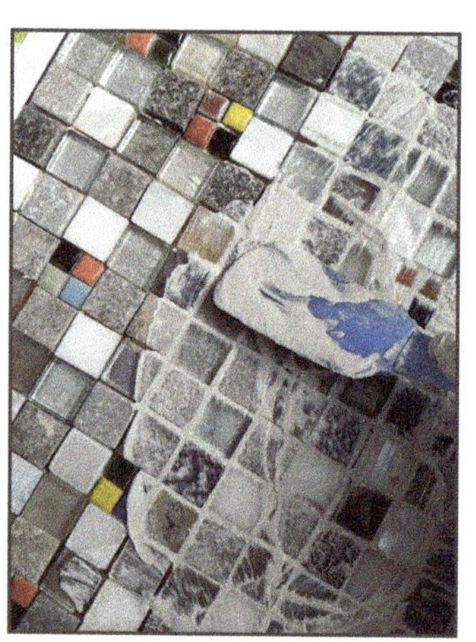

4 Prepare crème-colored grout according to the manufacture instructions and apply it on the tile using a spatula. Clean well and dry – that's it, the tile is ready!

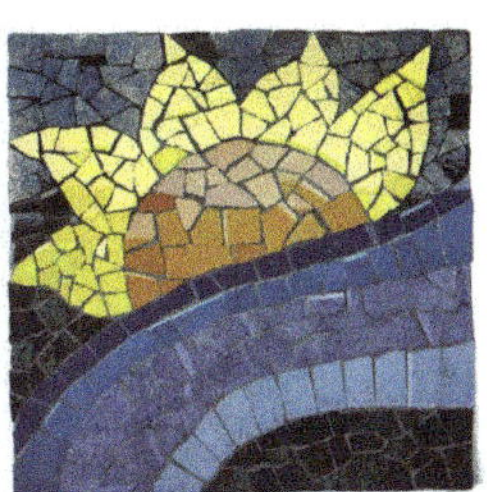

Tile no.2

A sun-like sunflower hiding behind a blue-hued wave. This tile combines two different styles of cuts from colorful ceramic tiles – straight cuts for the wave lines as well as various shapes. You can make this tile into an entire series if you change the direction of the wave and colors of the flower each time.

Since these are steppingstones, it's important that all the tiles you choose for this piece will be at the same height, to achieve a tile that is as straight as possible.

Materials:

Thick ceramic tile measuring 30x30 cm/11.8x11.8"
Ceramic tiles in tones of yellow, orange, several blue hues
Ceramics tile cutter
Wooden stick or spatula for applying the glue
A thin screwdriver or toothpick for cleaning excess glue
Tile glue
A small glue bowl
Light colored grout
Grout Gear: Mixing bowl, water, a wooden stick, rags, gloves

1 Copy the sample onto the ceramics using a copying paper. It's recommended to trace the painting with a permanent marker, so it doesn't get erased while gluing.

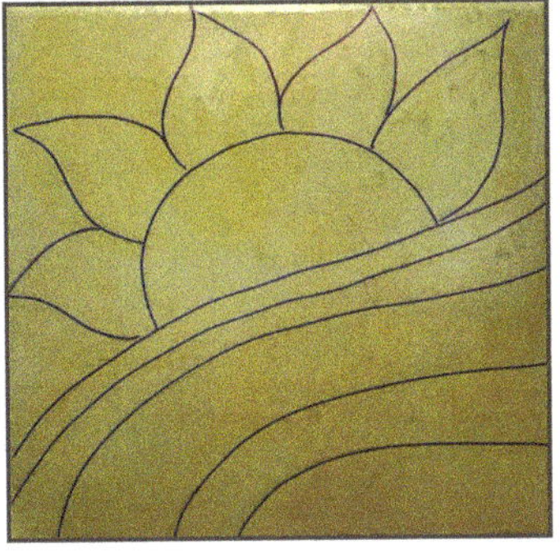

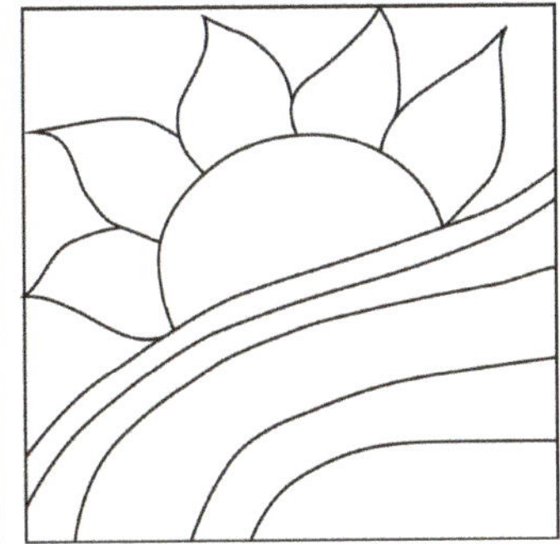

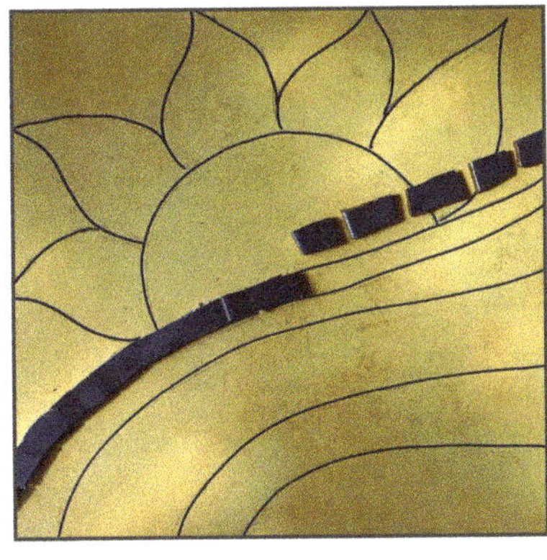

2 First blue stripe: Prepare a ceramic line at the right width (about a centimeter). You can cut it using a cutting machine or the tile cutting clamp (see cutting instructions). To receive a smooth and consecutive line, you should plan the tiling placement before gluing them on.

3 Do the second stripe in the same manner, in a lighter hue of blue. It's important to make sure the edge is straight as you reach the edge of the tile.

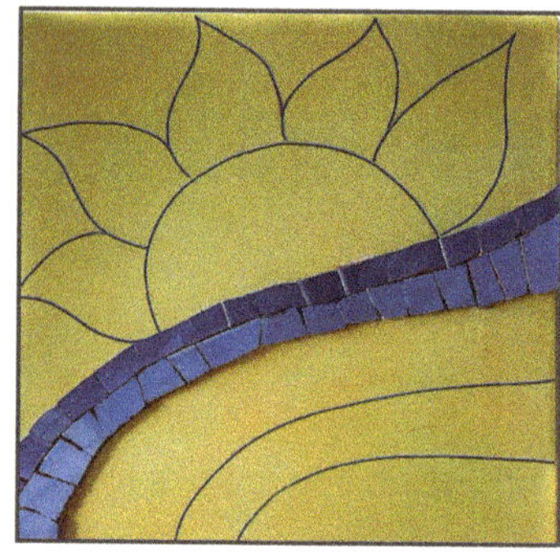

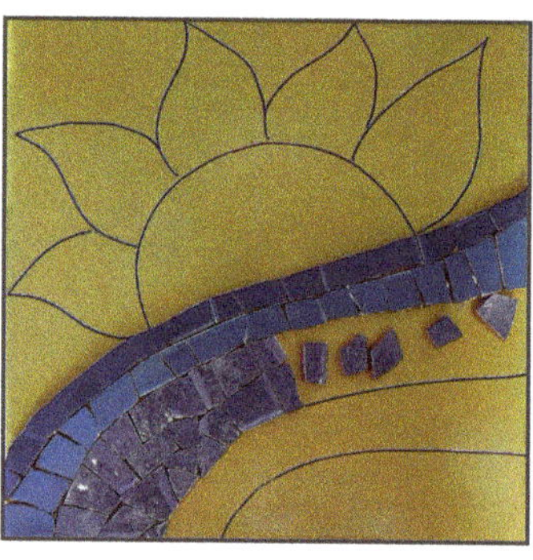

4 Cut a purple tile into random pieces and fill in the third wave.

5 The next stripe is made of straight light-blue ceramic pieces in different lengths. I've cut a stripe that's as wide as the thickest part and divided it into equal parts using the tile cutting clamp. I then marked with a marker and fit the length of each part into its right place, to keep a steady line.

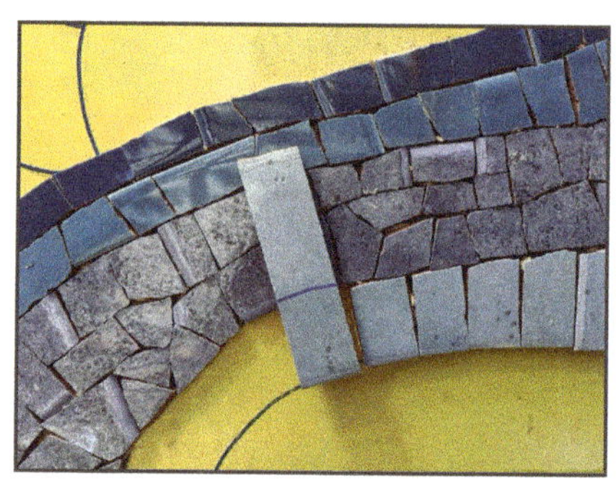

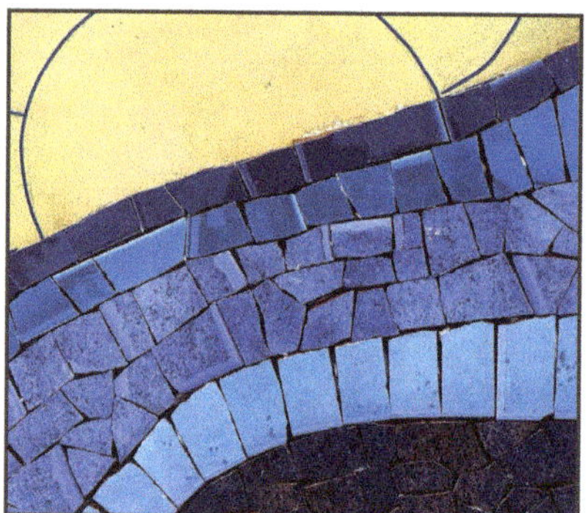

6 The last part of the wave is made of a dark-blue tile with a texture, cut to random pieces.

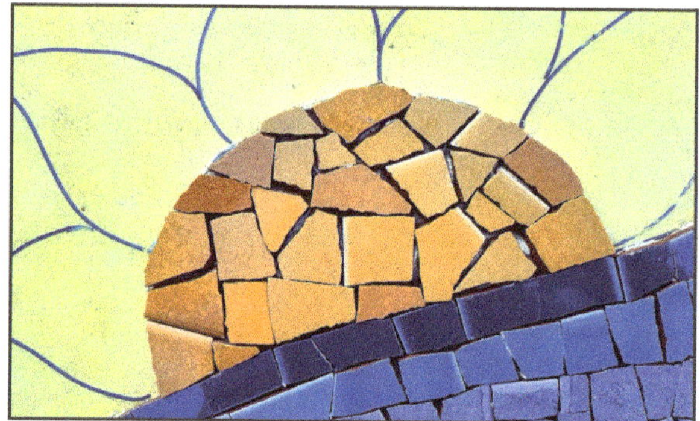

7 The sunflower: First, fill up the central part with orange-hue cut up tiles. It's important to make sure the arch is straight and without anything sticking out.

8 Petals: First, glue yellow triangles at the edge of each leaf to get a nice finish for the petals.

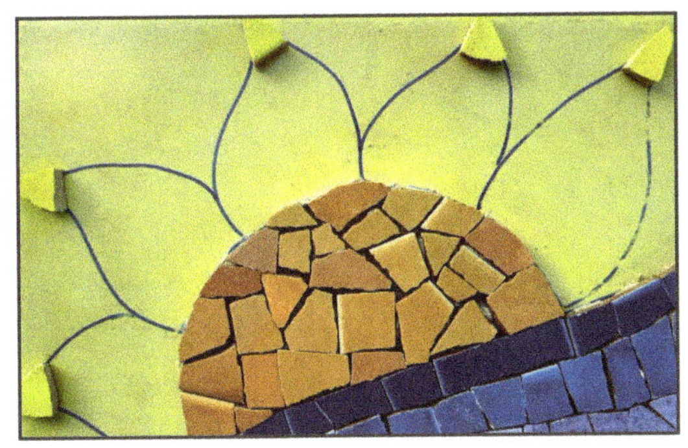

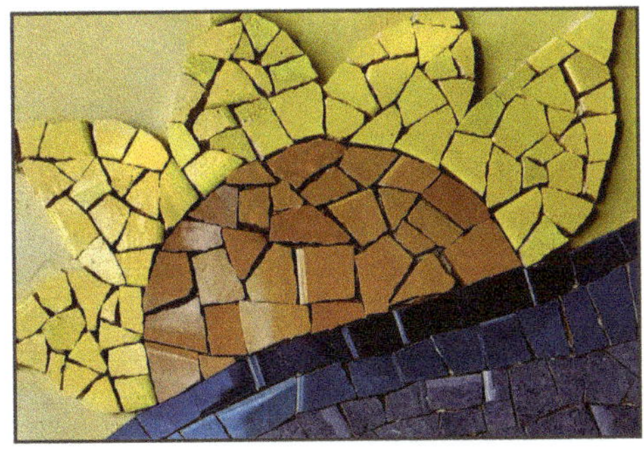

9 Fill in the petals with closely knitted yellow tile pieces.

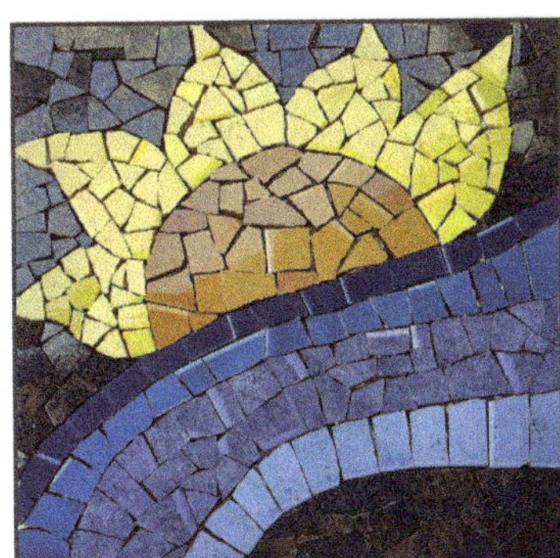

10 Complete the background with the dark blue, like the bottom wave.

11 Dry it for a day and prepare a dark-grey grout, according to manufacture instructions. Apply the tile with a spatula and notice that the grout gets into all the grooves.

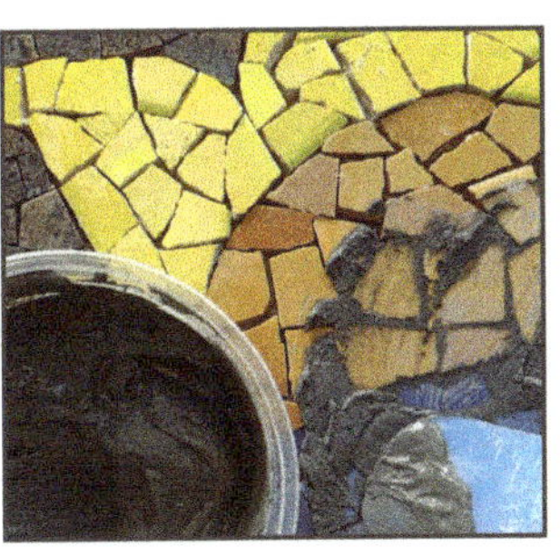

12 Clean and smooth it out to get a straight and smooth tile. And it's done!

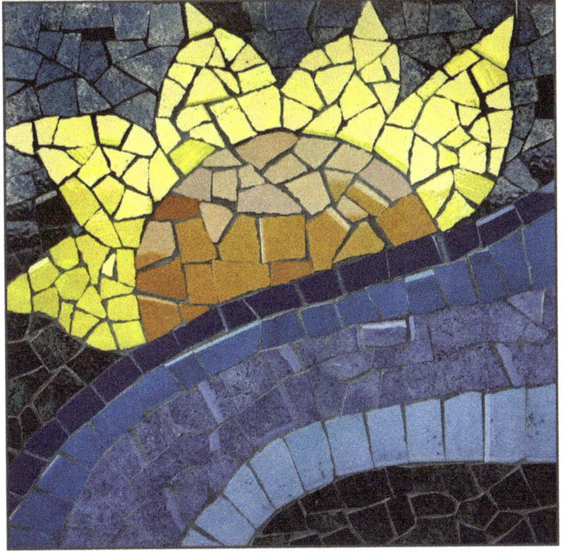

Tip: If there are any bumps left at the end, you can smoothen them out with the grout – fill in a bit more in certain places so the tile will be as smooth and straight as possible.

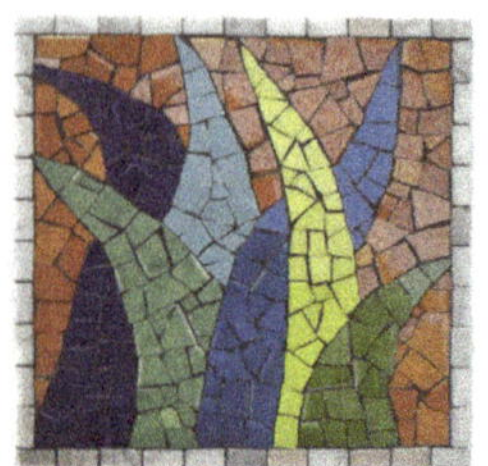

Tile no.3

Pointy leaves in blue and green shades on an orange background, combined with a natural stone frame.

It's also important here to make sure that all tiles are at the same height to have a tile that's as straight and smooth as possible.

Materials:

Thick ceramic tile measuring 30x30 cm/11.8x11.8"
Natural stone squares, 1.5x3 cm / 0.59x1.18"
Ceramic tiles: 3 shades of green; 3 shades of blue; orange for the background
A ceramic tile cutting clamp
Wooden stick or spatula
A thin screwdriver or toothpick for cleaning excess glue
Tile glue
A small glue bowl
Light colored grout
Grout Gear: Mixing bowl, water, a wooden stick, rags, gloves

1 Copy the sample onto the tile using a copying paper. It's recommended to trace the painting with a permanent marker, so it doesn't get erased while gluing.

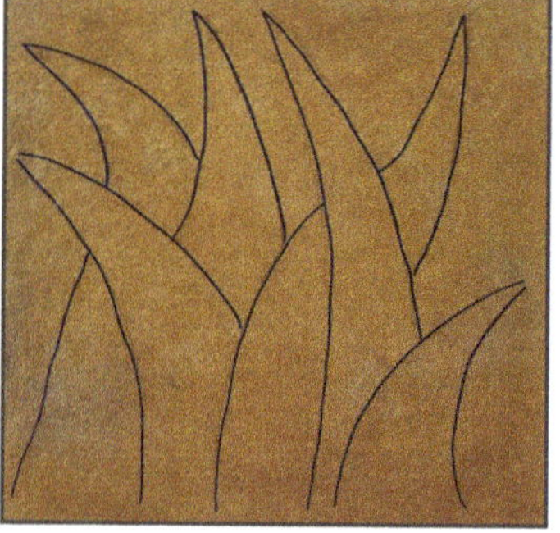

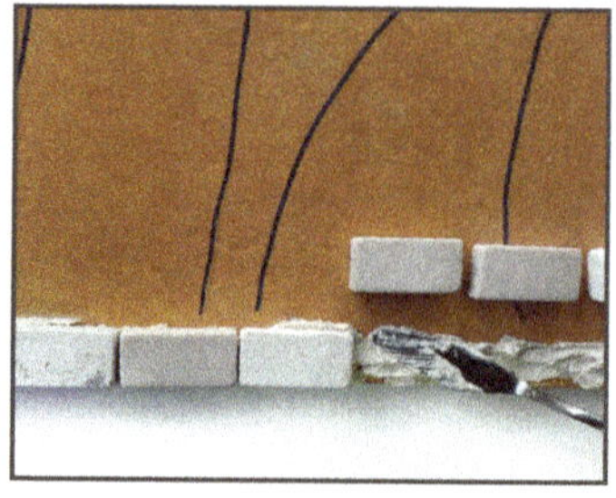

2 Start from the frame. Glue the rectangles close to the edge in a straight and closely knitted manner. You can apply a line of glue with the spatula or stick and glue the rectangles onto it.

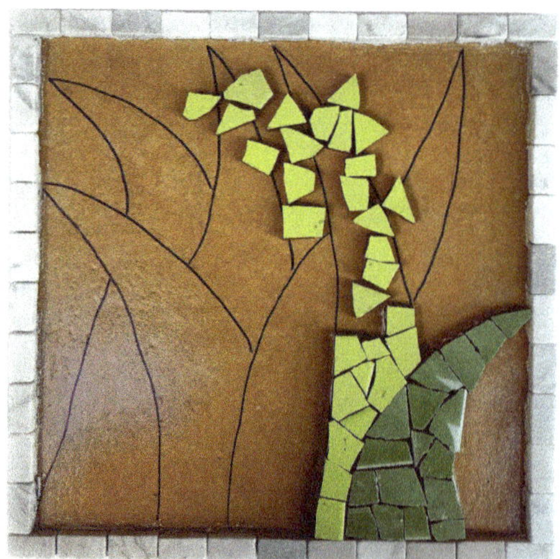

3 Cut the tiles into random shapes and start gluing the leaves, from right to left – the right one should be dark green, then light green. Make sure to glue precisely and relatively closely-knit.

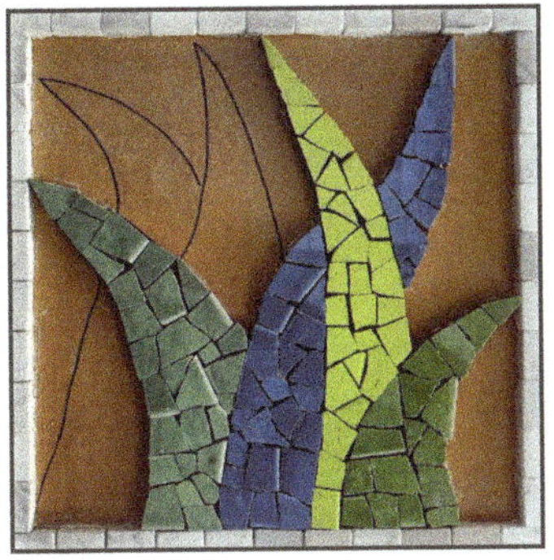

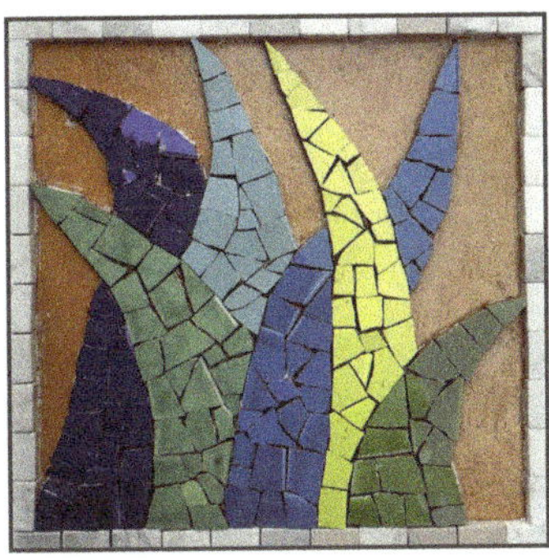

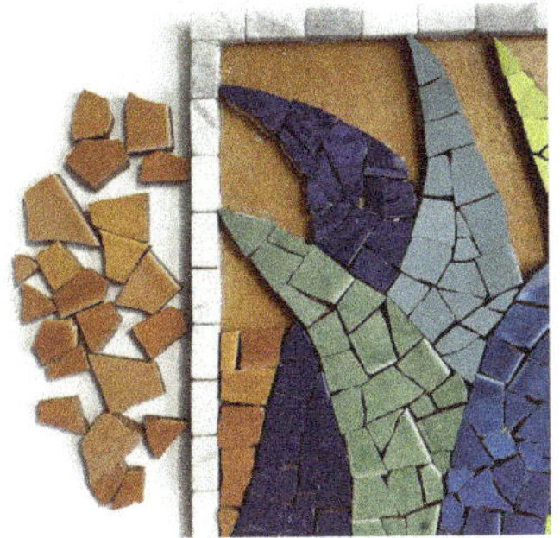

4 The third leaf – blue and then another green one.

5 Complete the two remaining leaves in blue and light blue colors.

6 Cut an orange tile into random shapes and fill in the remaining background.

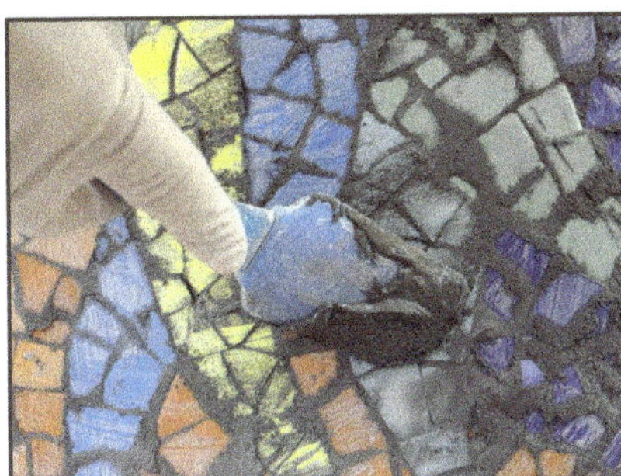

7 Wait a day for it to dry and prepare dark-grey grout, according to manufacture instructions. Apply it to the tile using a spatula and make sure the grout gets into all the grooves.

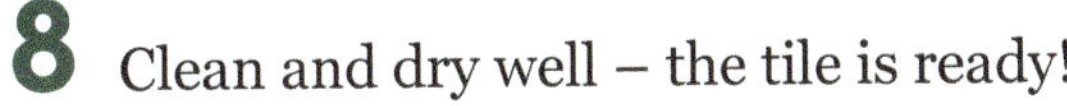

8 Clean and dry well – the tile is ready!

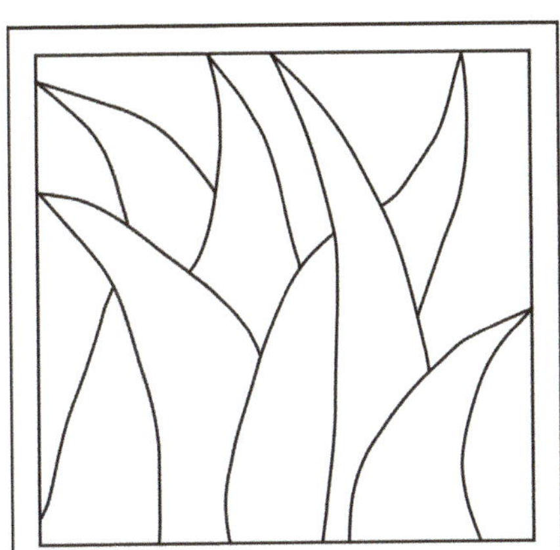

Pattern for the tile:
Enlarge on a photocopier according to the tile size.

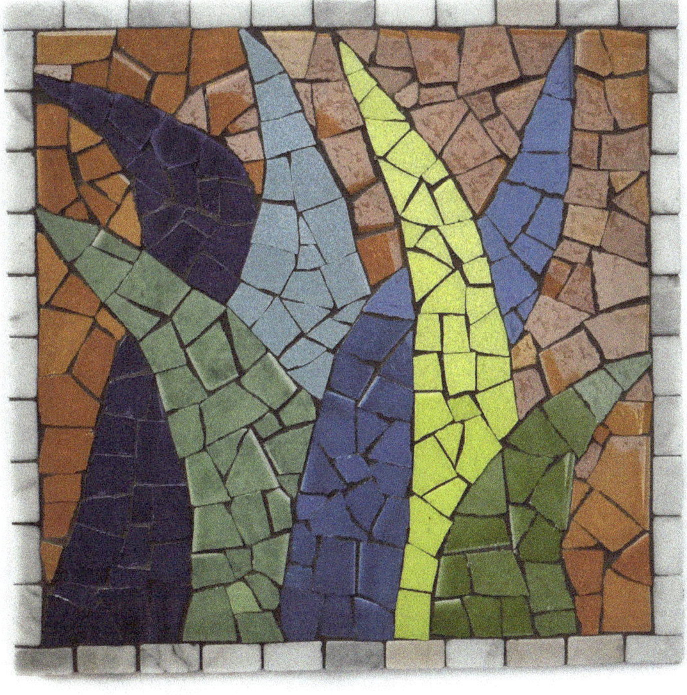

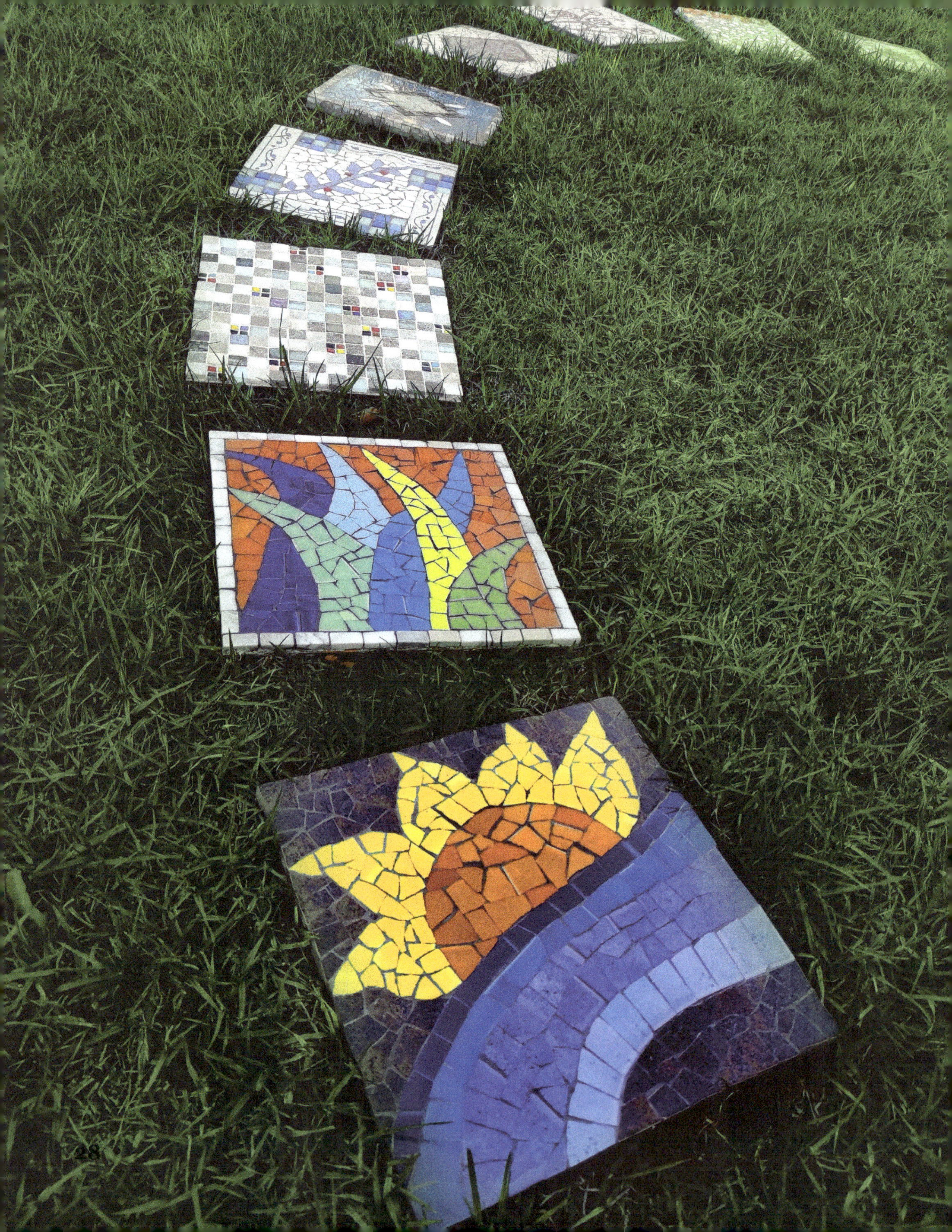

Using the Mosaic Cutter

Before cutting, wear safety goggles to protect your eyes from small fragments.

1 Hold the bottom of the cutter with your dominant hand, with the curved side facing toward the ceramic. Hold the ceramic tile in your other hand, and in your dominant hand, hold the bottom of the cutter handle.

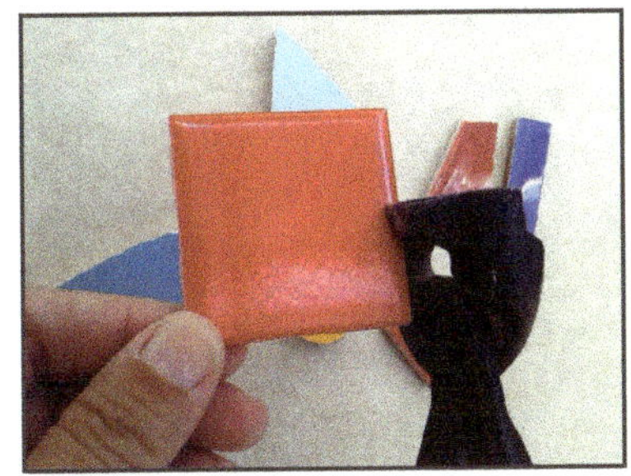

2 Hold the ceramic tile with the cutter in a straight or diagonal orientation for the type of crop you want, and clip!

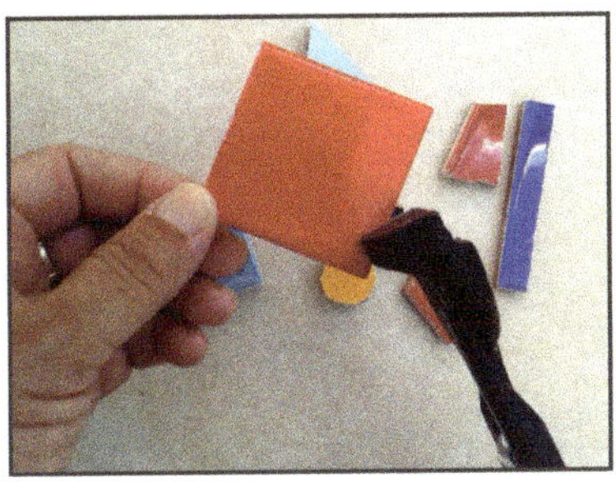

3 If you want to cut small pieces or shape the tile, hold the tile by the widest part of the cutter and clip.

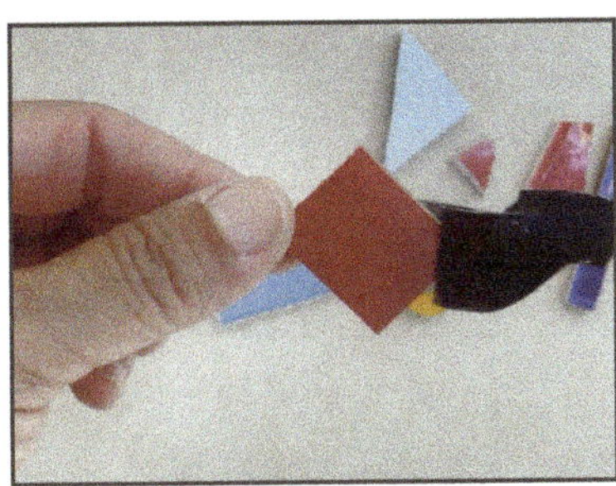

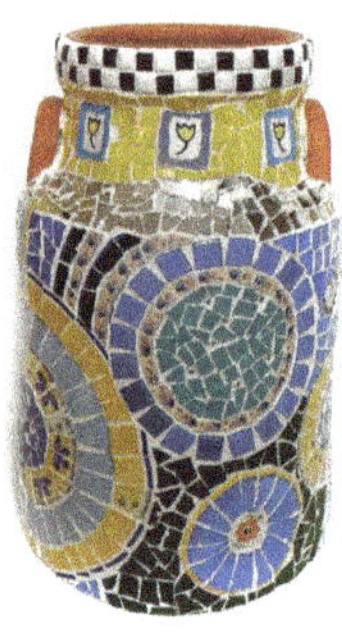

Project: Pot Plant out of Broken Plates

A large pot plant in the shape of a jug was given a renewed, heartfelt look using broken plates and mirrors. You can use this sample for any large pot plant you'd like to decorate with mosaic. It's an opportunity to take advantage of all those old or cracked plates you've gathered all these years and even ask some from your neighbors, so you can get all the right shades. Use the wheeled glass nipper for cutting, see instructions and explanations ahead.

Glue all the pieces with tile glue so that the finished pot plant will be able to withstand any weather outdoors.

Materials:

A tall pot plant, at least 40 cm / 15.7"
Plates with a peripheral pattern in shades of yellow, blue and green
Glass squares in shades of black and white, 1x1 cm / 0.39"
Mirrors
Wheeled glass nipper
Tile glue
Wooden spatula or stick for applying the glue
A think screwdriver or toothpick to clean off excess glue
A small glue bowl
Light grout
Grout Gear: Mixing bowl, water, a wooden stick, rags, gloves

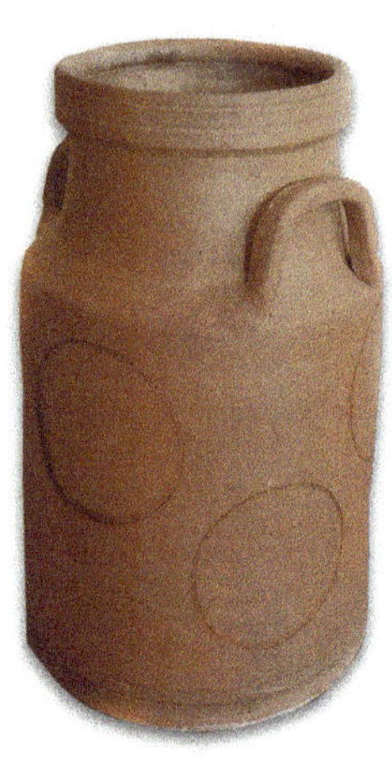

1 Using a round plate and marker, paint different sized circles on the pot plant.

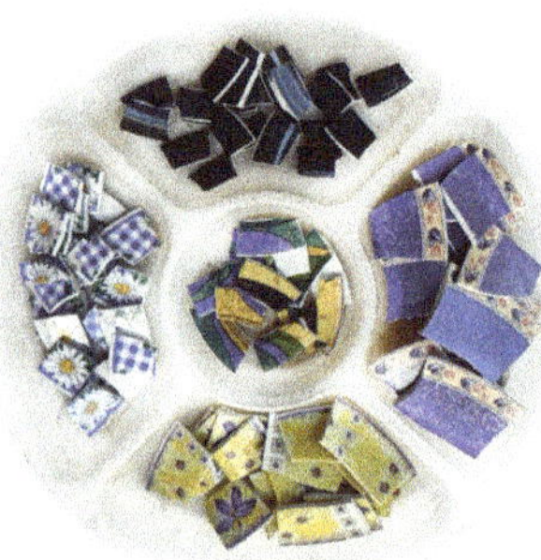

2 Prepare plate pieces broken into rectangles beforehand, made of the frames of blue and yellow shaded plates (see explanation on how to cut the plates with the wheeled nipper).

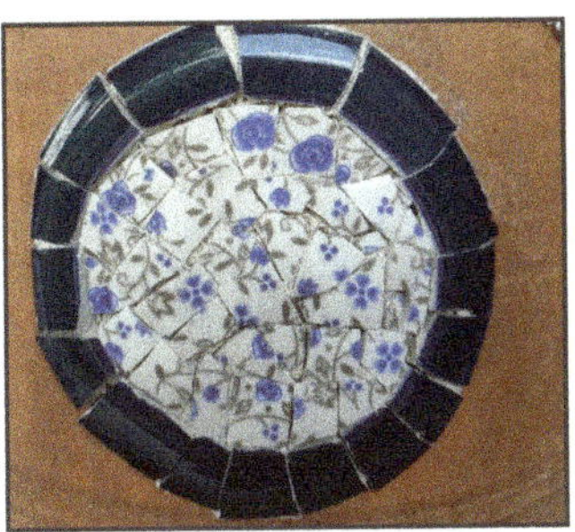

3 Glue the frame of the cut plate as a circle contour. Make different-colored circles around the pot plant.

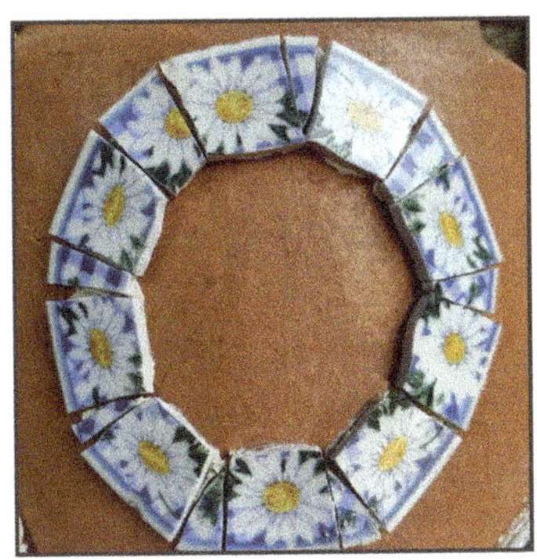

4 Fill the inside of the circles with different shades, cut into small random pieces.

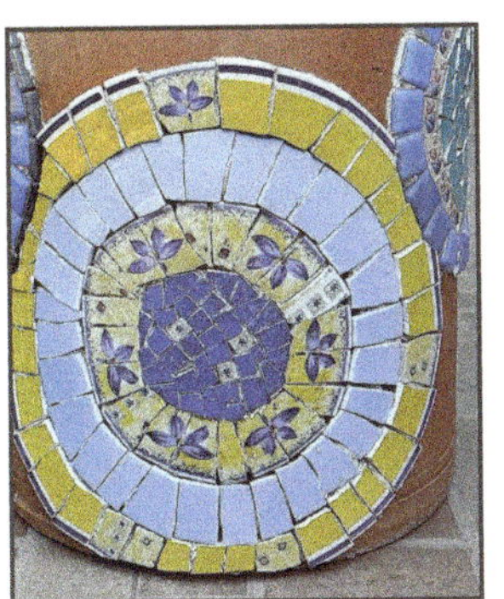

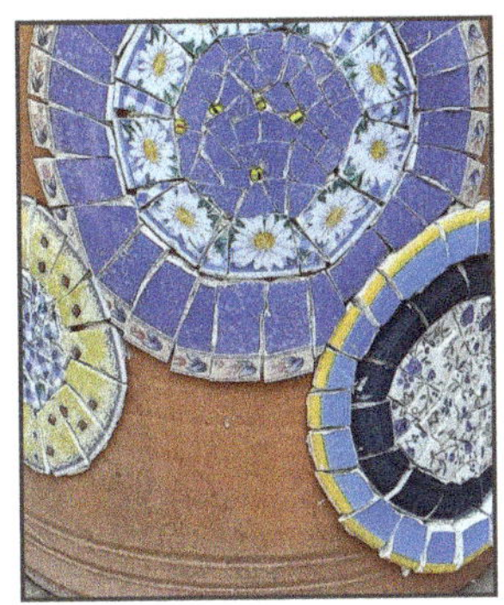

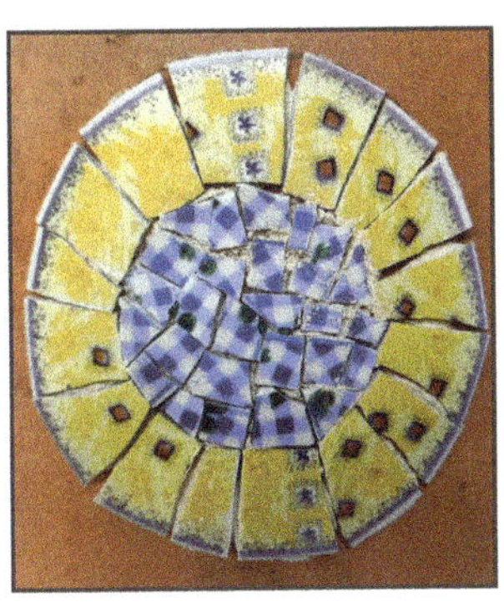

5 Do the same thing until the entire pot plant is full of colorful circles.

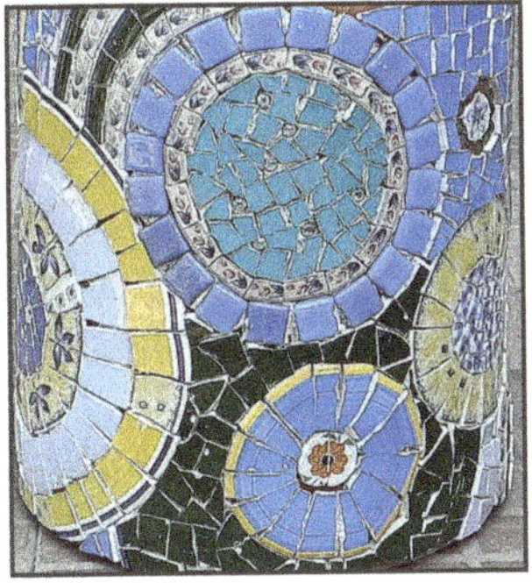

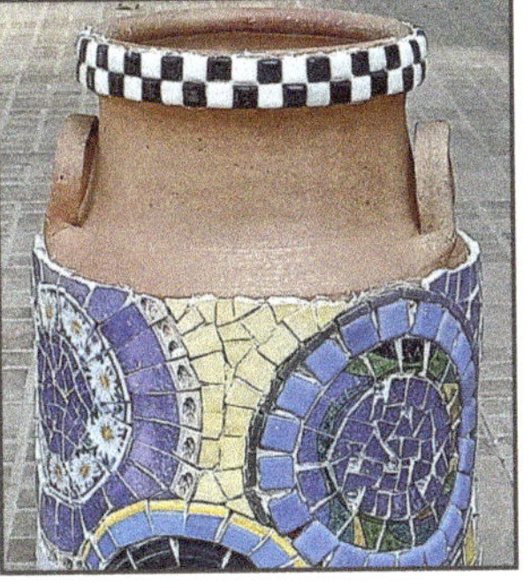

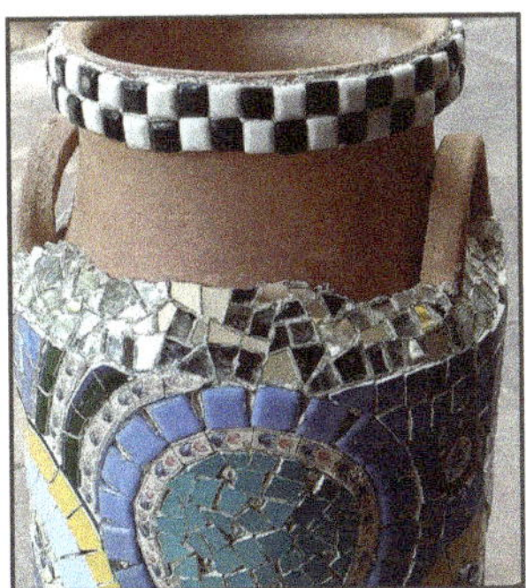

6 Fill the background with the plate pieces. Here I chose green to bring out the bluish, yellowish shades.

7 Stick two lines of black and white squares at the top of the pot plant.

8 Add a wide line of cut mirrors.

9 Fill in the gap created between the plate pieces. In this example there is a combination of flowers cut from plates, along with yellow plate pieces.

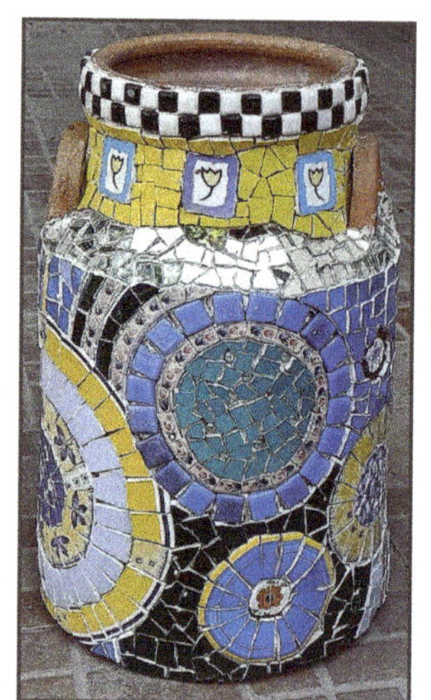

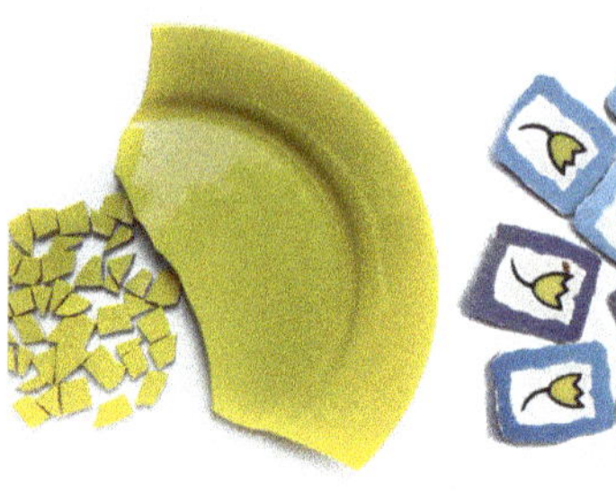

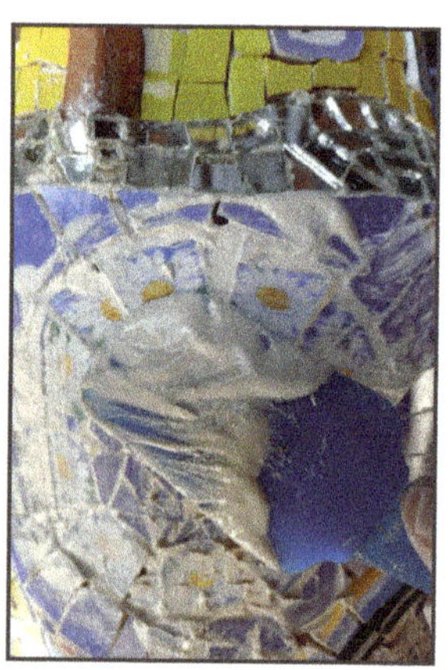

10 Wait at least a day for it to dry and make creme-colored grout according to the instructions. Apply the grout on the pot plant using a spatula. It's very important to make time, before starting the grout process, since there might be height differences between plates and many small places to clean.

11 The pot plant is ready! You can polish the mirrors with a window cleaning liquid or a damp wipe, and of course, look for a plant that fits.

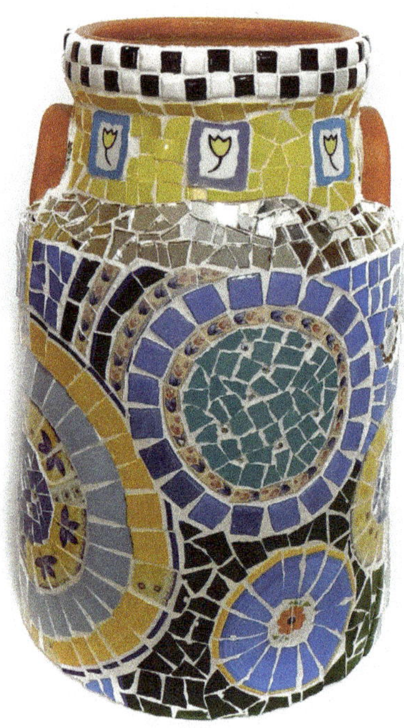

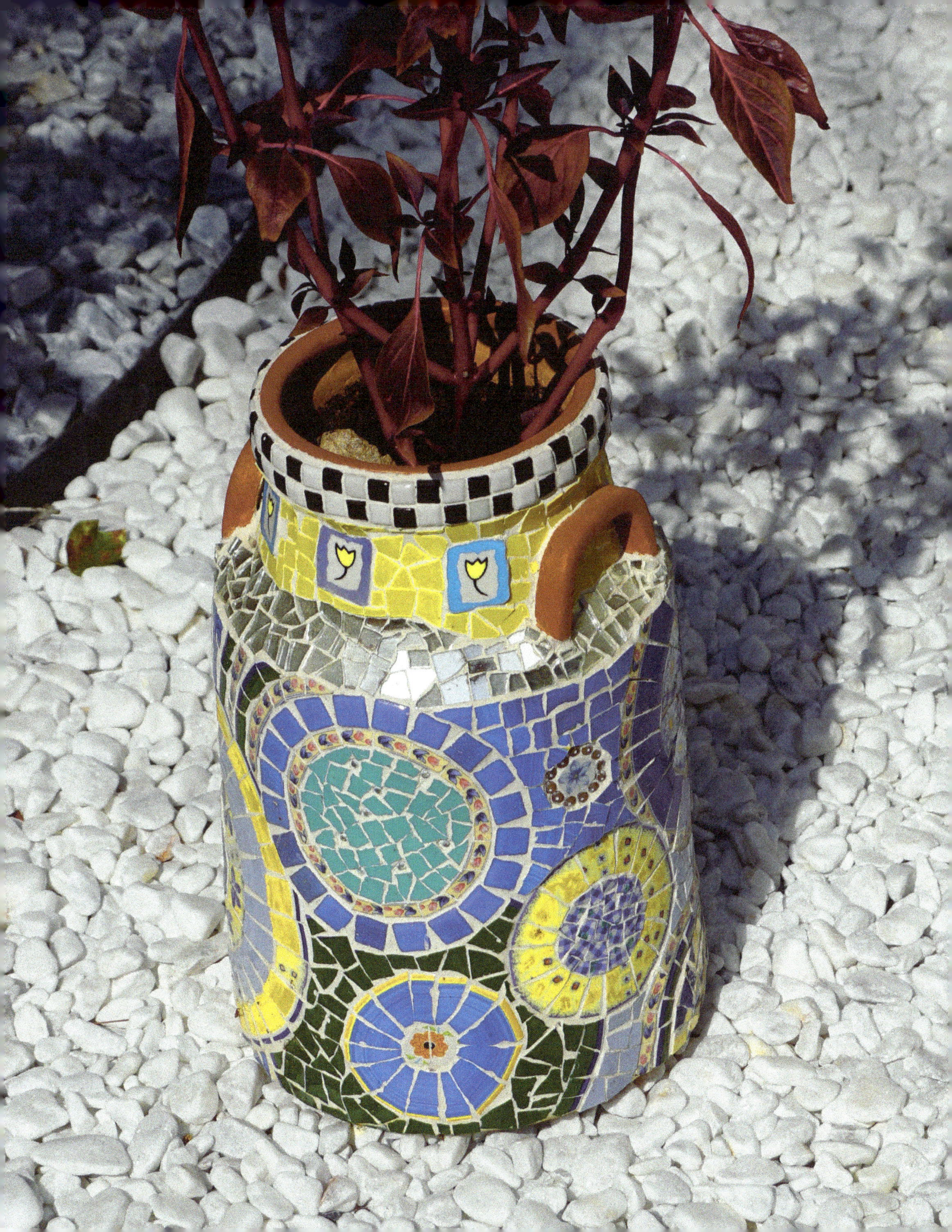

Cutting Mugs and Cups using a Wheeled Nipper

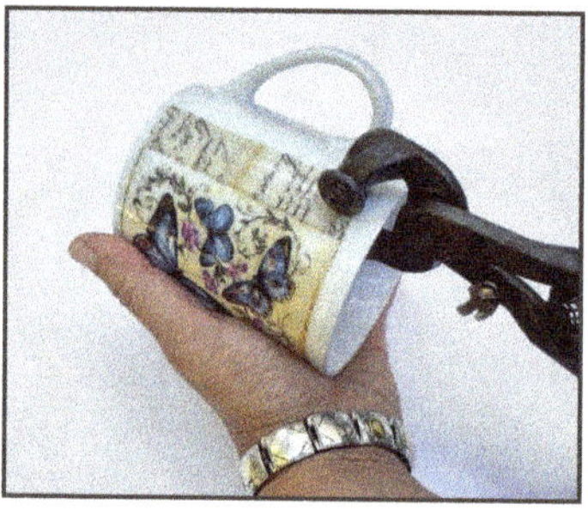

1 Hold the nipper with your dominant hand and support the piece with your other hand. Bring the nipper to the rim, with the wheels clutching it from both sides.

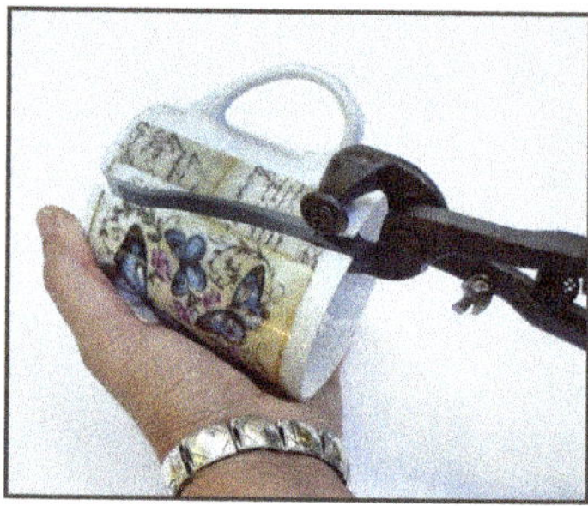

2 Firmly press the nipper until the piece is cut.

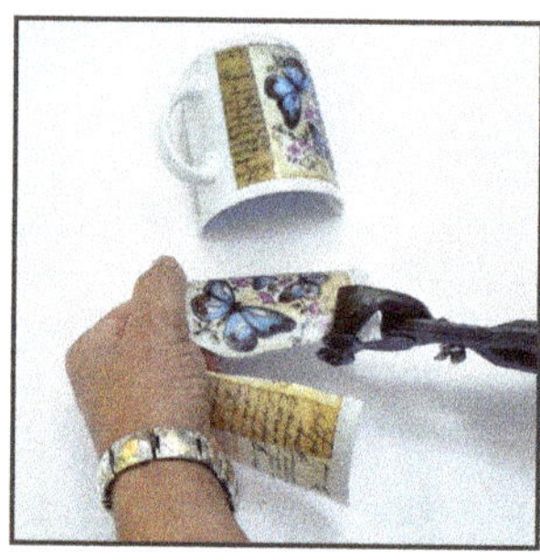

3 Keep cutting the parts of the mug using the nipper.

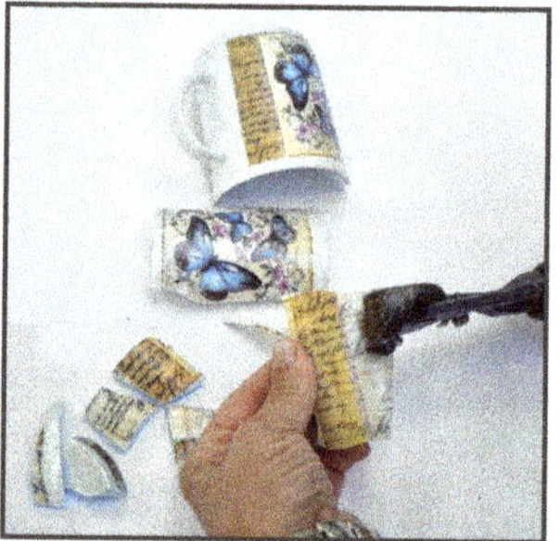

4 Remove excess parts and reduce them to the desired size.

Cutting a plate using a wheeled nipper

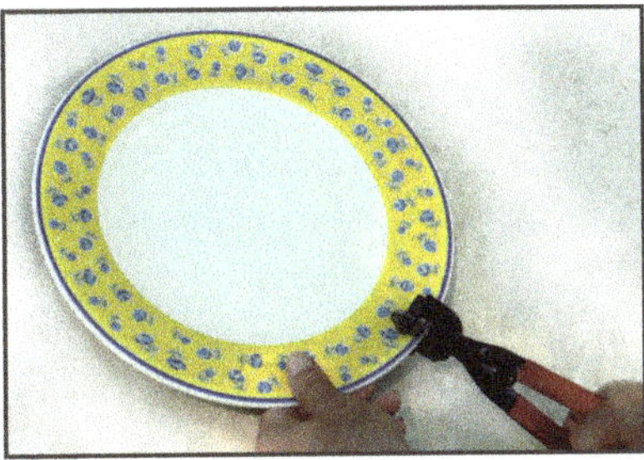

1 Hold on to the nipper with your dominant hand and the plate with the other.

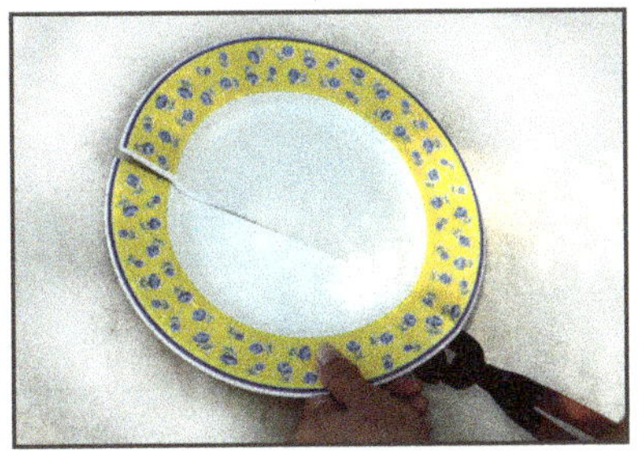

2 Put the nipper closer to the center of the plate, with the wheels clutching it on both sides, and click. The wheels will cut the plate.

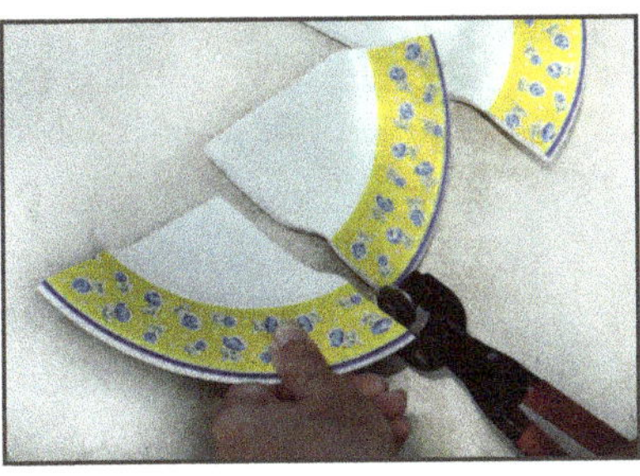

3 Keep cutting the plate to quarters in the same way, then to smaller pieces.

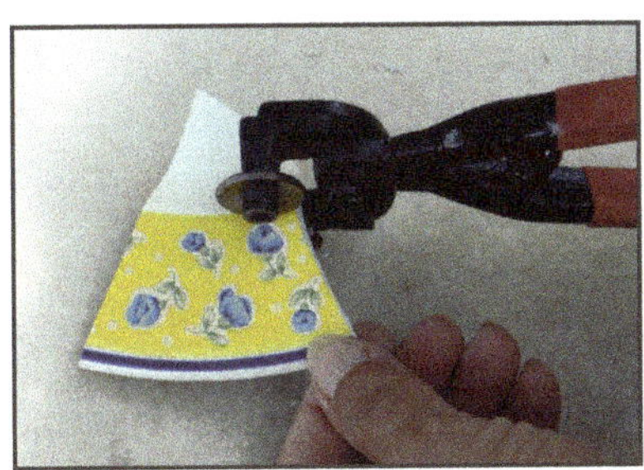

4 When the parts are smaller you can easily take off the excess by cutting them again.

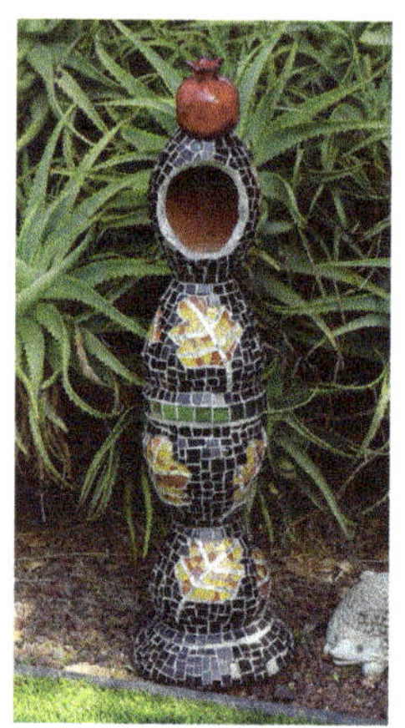

Project: Pot Plant Totem

It's sometimes hard to find a very tall pot plant to decorate the yard, but you can put together and make one on your own. The totem is made of several different-sized pot plants, glued together from different sides.

When choosing the pot plants, it's important to make sure they come together nicely, so the pasting will be steady, and the totem will look complete. Another thing to notice is that all pot plants have a hole in the bottom, so you can pass a pole through them and stabilize the totem at its location.

The bottom pot plant can be glued to a coaster/an upside-down ceramic plate, or any other round and sturdy surface, so you can stabilize the totem and get a wide and heavy base. You should also make a hole in the center of that base.

Materials:

4 pot plants that can connect to one another + a coaster/ceramic plate
Mirrors
Black ceramics
Glass in shades of yellow, brown and orange
Black 1 cm / 0.39" squares
A 1 cm / 0.39" iron pole in diameter, longer than the length of the totem
Wheeled nipper
Ceramic cutting nipper
Glass cutting equipment: knife, ruler, and breaking nipper
A wooden stick or spatula
A thin screwdriver or toothpick to clean the excess glue
Tile glue
Silicone glue or super glue
A small glue bowl
Crème-colored grout
Grout Gear: Mixing bowl, water, a wooden stick, rags, gloves

1 Prepare a few pot plants that can connect to one another, including a coaster.

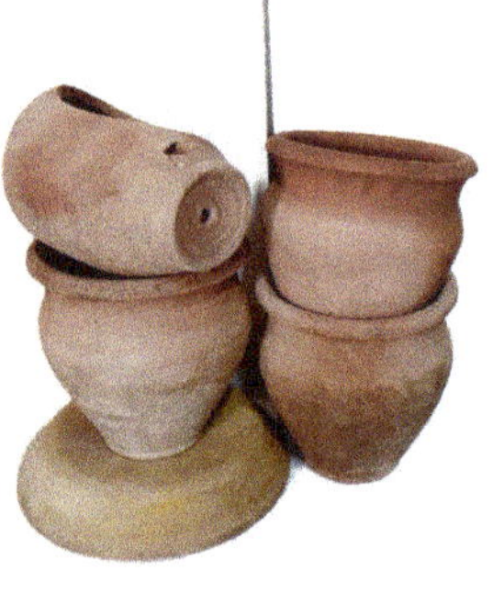

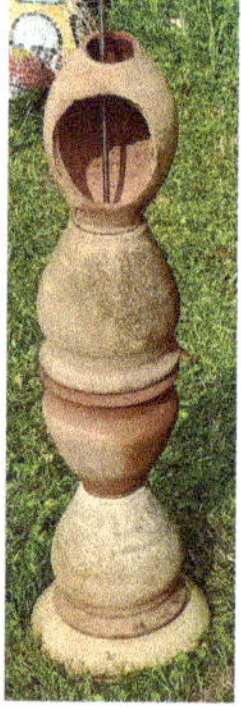

2 Make sure that the pot plants are well-connected and mark them with numbers at their contact points.

3 The first pot plant is glued upside-down to the coaster/wide plate. Using a marker, paint 2-3 leaves on each pot plant separately, depending on its size.

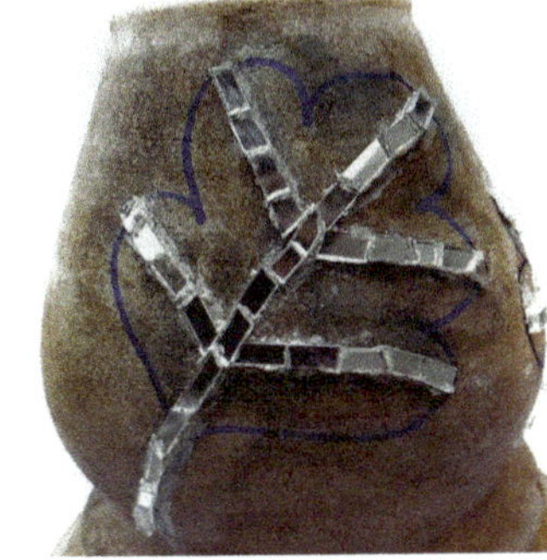

4 Using a glass cutting knife and a ruler, cut thin stripes of glass (about 1 cm /0.39" thick). Cut each strip into smaller pieces, using the nipper, and glue it on the leaves' veins. Do the same for all the pot plants making up the totem.

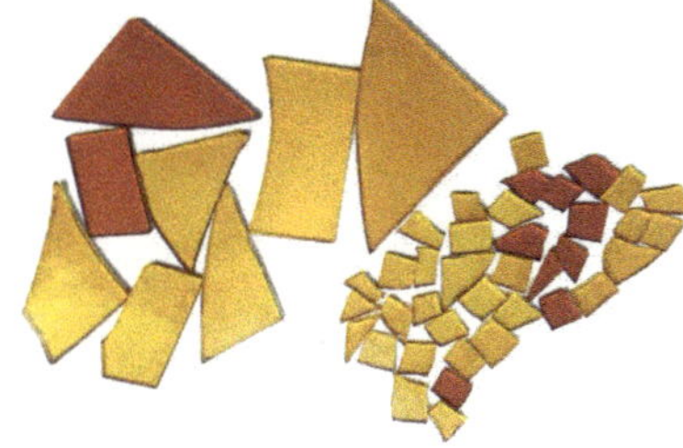

5 Cut yellow-brown glass into small pieces.

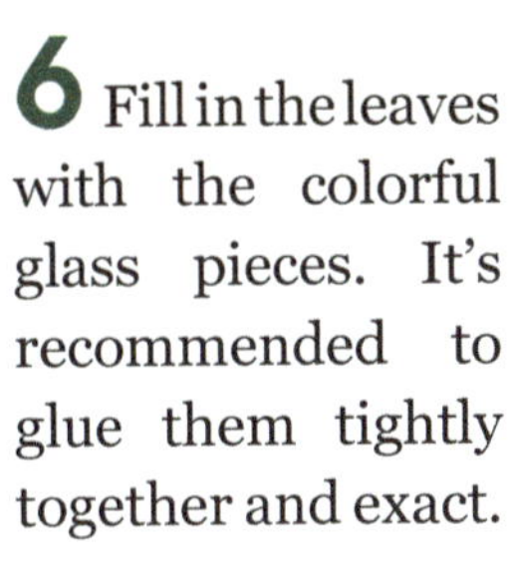

6 Fill in the leaves with the colorful glass pieces. It's recommended to glue them tightly together and exact.

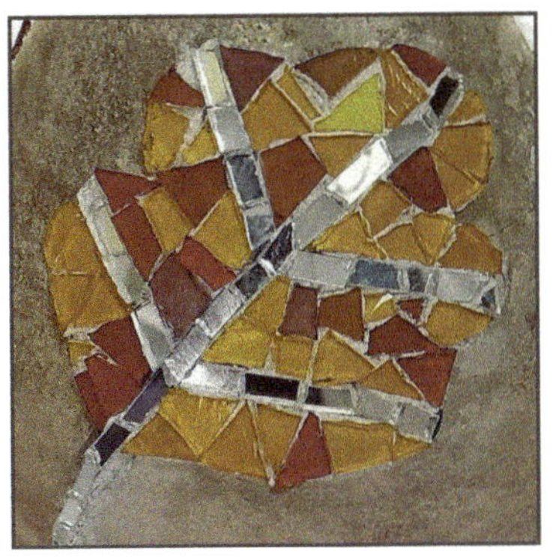

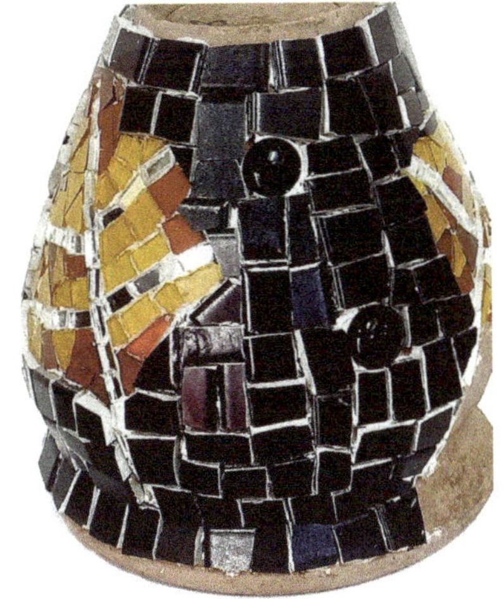

7 Cut black ceramics into squares and rectangles and fill up the background. You can combine black nuggets between them.

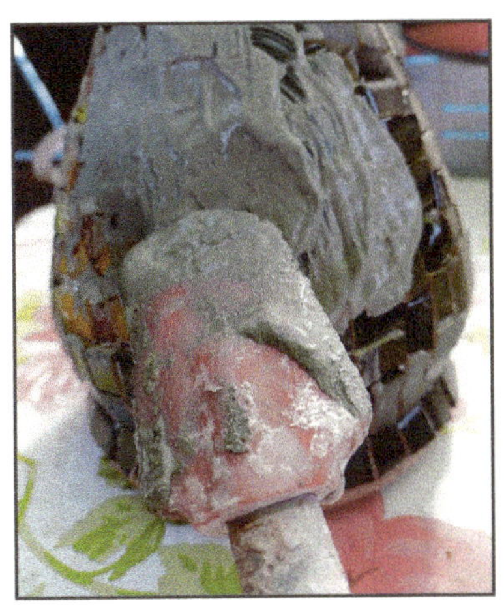

8 Once all the pot plant are covered in black mosaic, you can make the grout for each pot plant separately. Clean well with a wet towel.

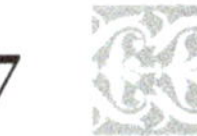

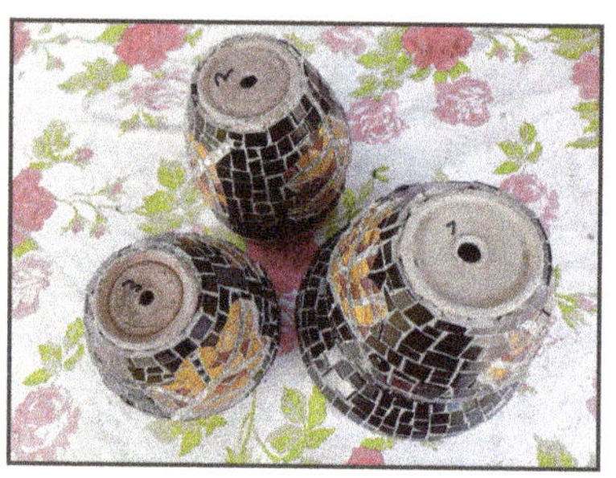

9 Prepare the pot plants to be glued together – make sure you have the right order to create the totem.

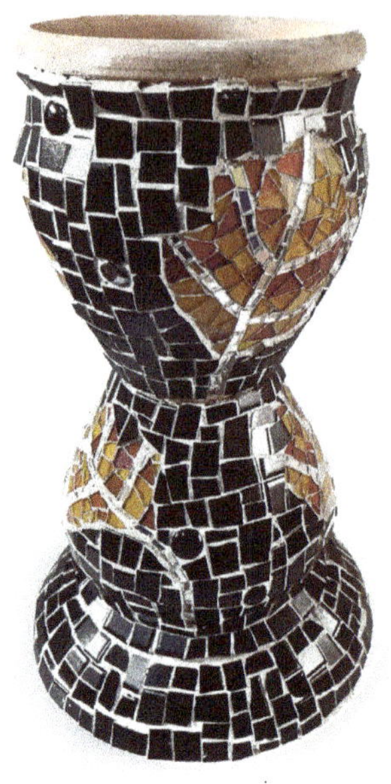

10 Glue the pot plant together using a strong and quick adhesive.

11 Using the same adhesive, glue black squares to cover the connections and leave to dry. When needed, complete the grout in the missing spaces a few hours or a day later.

Set the totem in its place, you can finish it with an open pot plant and plant or a closed one and a decoration. In case it's not heavy or sturdy enough, you should run an iron pole through it, connected to the ground.

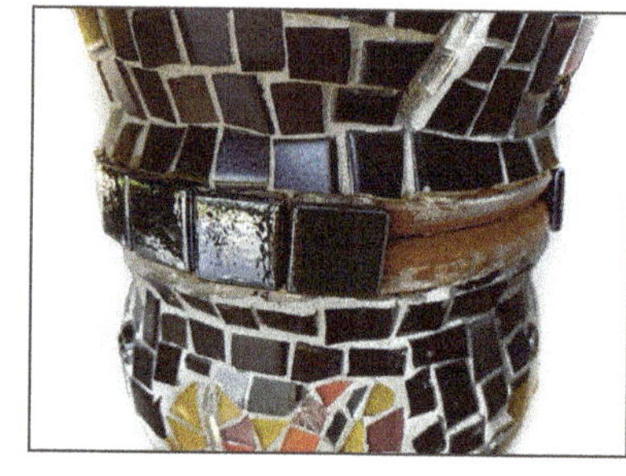

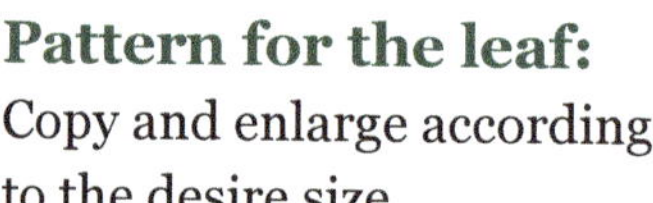

Pattern for the leaf:
Copy and enlarge according to the desire size.

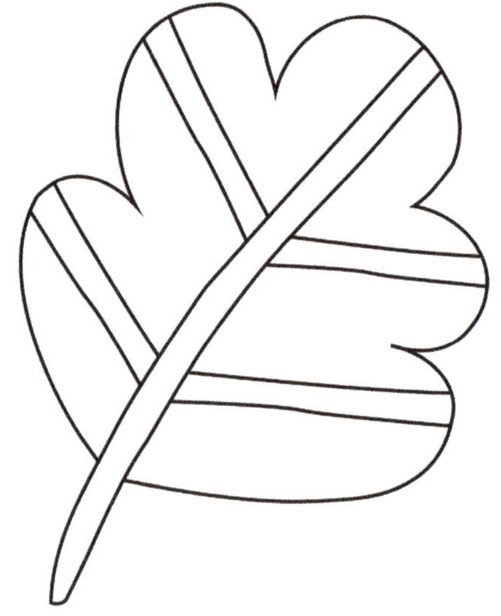

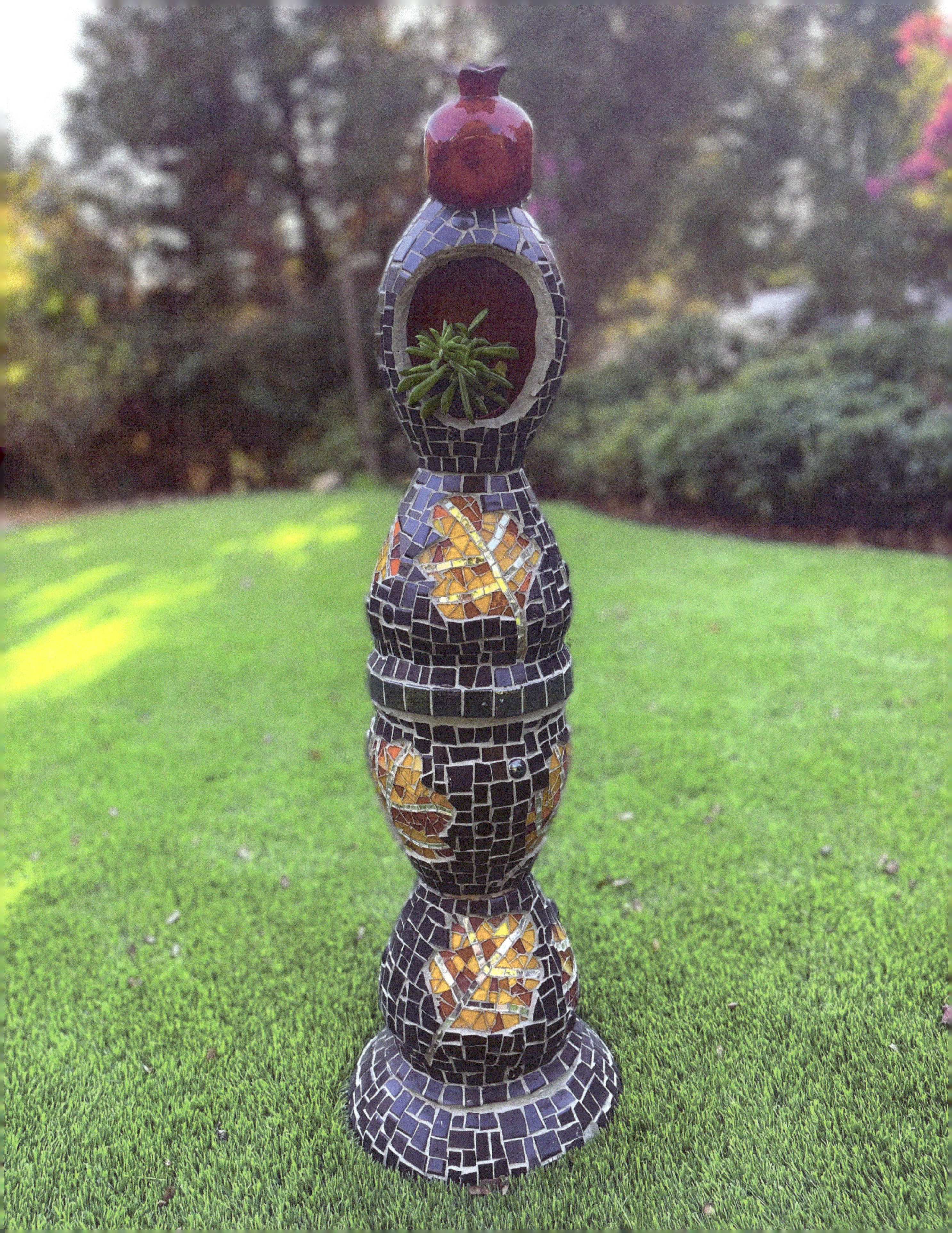

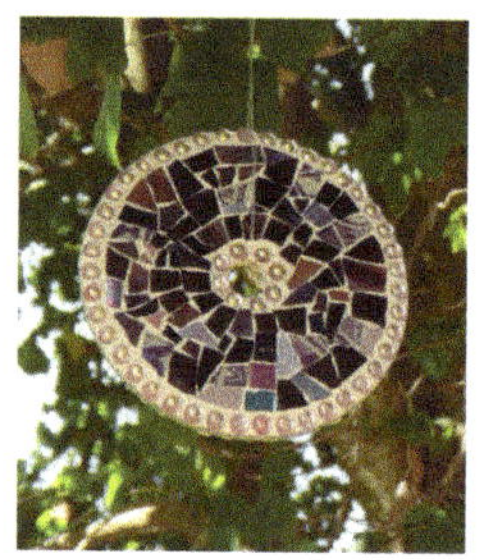

Project: Suspended Disks

Remember how we used to listen to music? We had records, cassettes, CDs... nowadays everything is electronic, we listen to music through our computers or phones. What do we do with all those CDs we gathered through the years? We coat them with mosaic and hang them on plants in the garden! This way, we recycle the CDs and not throw them away, and maybe get a happy and colorful decoration in the process. I'd like to show you something very easy to make.

Materials:

2 old CDs
Different-colored glass
Small, flat circles
Wheeled nipper
A wooden stick or spatula for applying glue
A thin screwdriver or toothpick to clean excess glue
Tile glue
Silicone glue or super glue
A small glue bowl
Crème-colored grout
Grout Gear: Mixing bowl, water, a wooden stick, rags, gloves

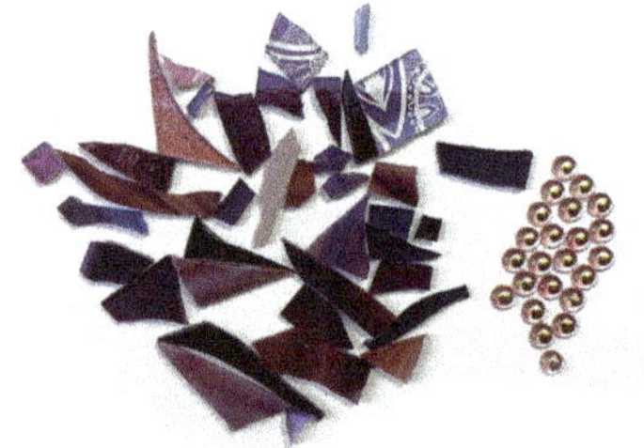

1 Cut colorful glass into small pieces.

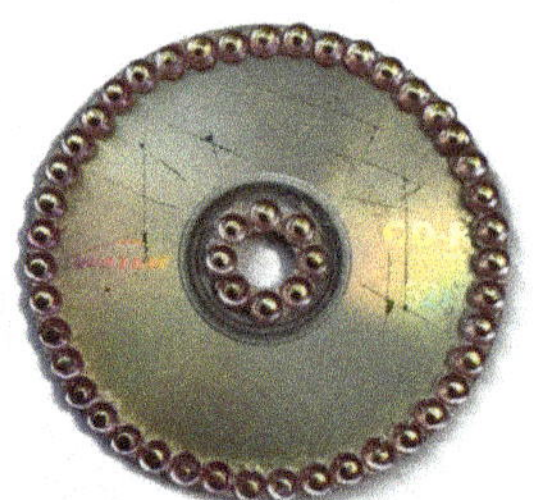

2 Using tile glue, glue flat semi-circles at the outer and inner rims of the disc.

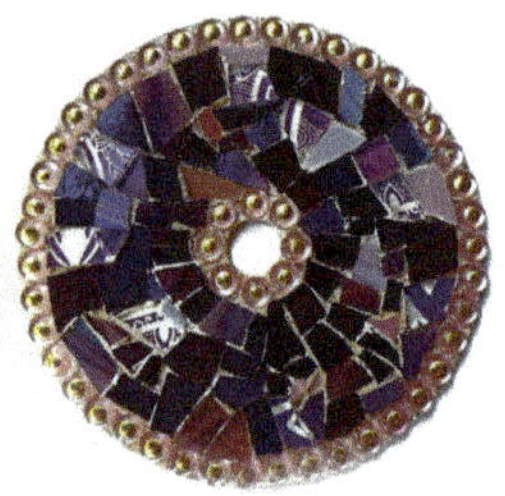

3 Glue the cut glass onto the surface of the disc.

4 Wait for it to dry and in the meantime glue glass on a different disc. You can coat each one with a different shade of glass.

5 Once both discs are dry (takes about a day), prepare grout according to instructions. Glue both discs to one another using super glue and hang using a thick and see-through fishing line.

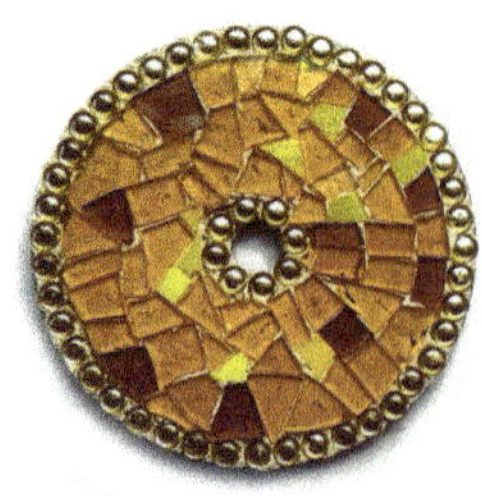

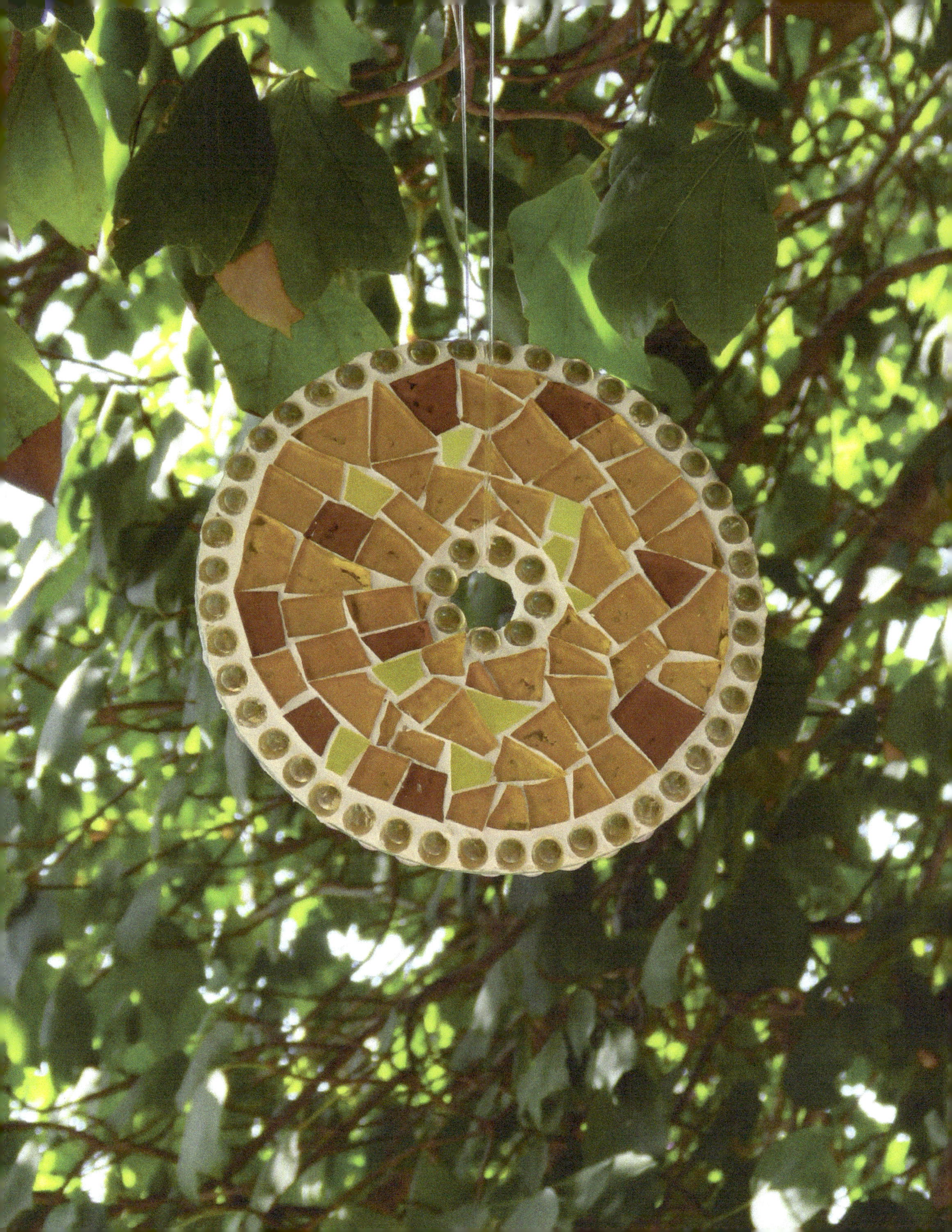

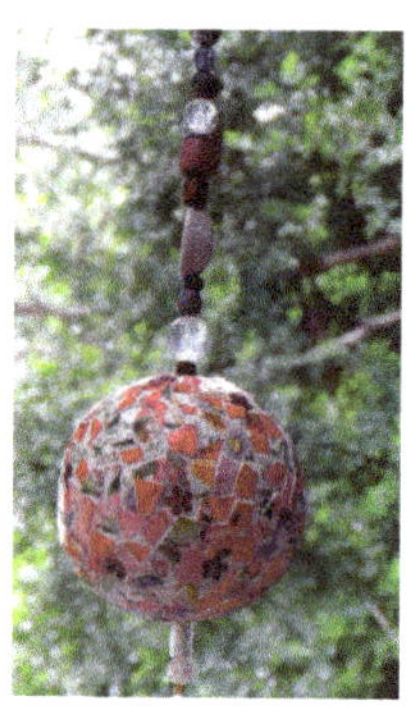

Project: Suspended Mosaic Spheres

If you have trees in your garden, you can suspend decorations from them. It can be glass bells, chains, discs – like the previous project – and colorful and happy mosaic spheres. The base for this piece is polystyrene, so it won't be too heavy, and the covering materials are versatile, as you'd like.

Below are five examples for different spheres, each in a completely different style. The materials are glass, different shades and color squares, plate and cup shards, mirrors, and beads. There are endless ideas and patterns that you can apply, whatever you can image and feel like.

You can suspend the spheres or place them on a metal rod, whatever you do, it's important to prepare the infrastructure beforehand, as to not damage the mosaic. I think this is a fun piece and a wonderful decoration for any garden.

Base:

Materials:

Polystyrene sphere
Mosaic fiberglass mesh cut into little pieces
Tile glue
Metal spatula for applying the glue
Wooden spikes

1 Pass the wooden spike across the polystyrene sphere, right at the center.

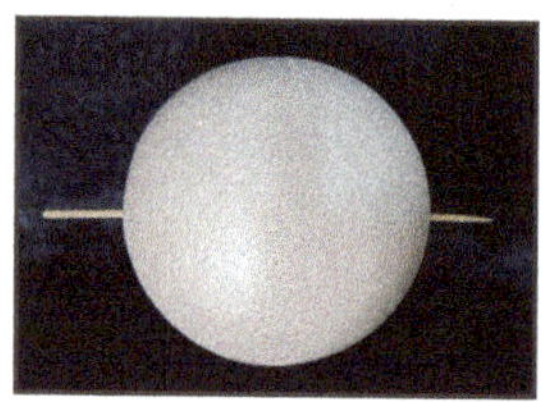

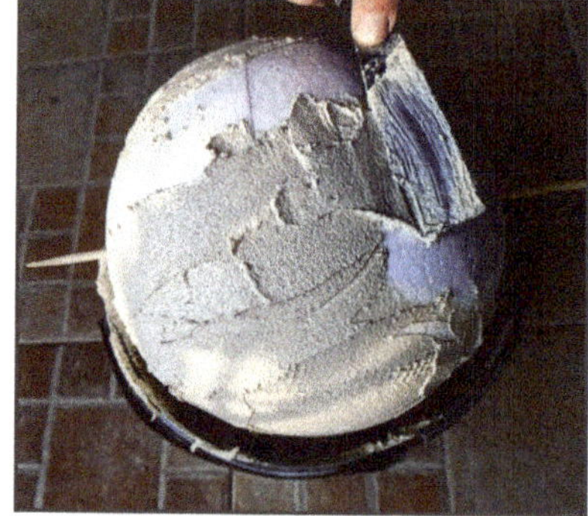

2 Place the polystyrene sphere on a slightly bigger bucket or bowl, so you could rotate it and apply glue without touching it. using the spatula, apply a thin layer of tile glue on the sphere.

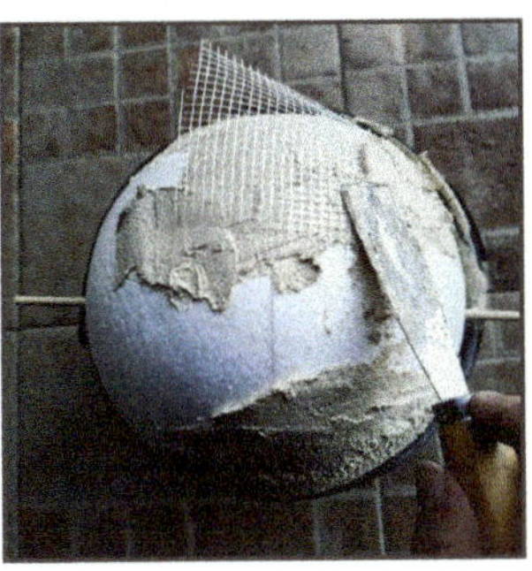

3 Place small pieces of mesh on the sphere and apply the glue on top of it well. The mesh is meant for strengthening and better gluing. Keep coating the sphere this way, using the mesh and glue. Rotate the sphere around each time, as needed.

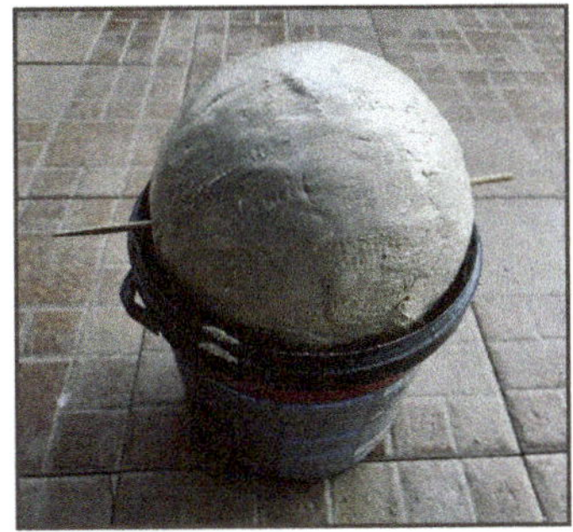

4 Smoothen the glue with a bit of water until you have a smooth sphere ready for pasting. Dry the sphere a bit before gluing the mosaic on. Leave the wooden spike in until you finish gluing the mosaic.

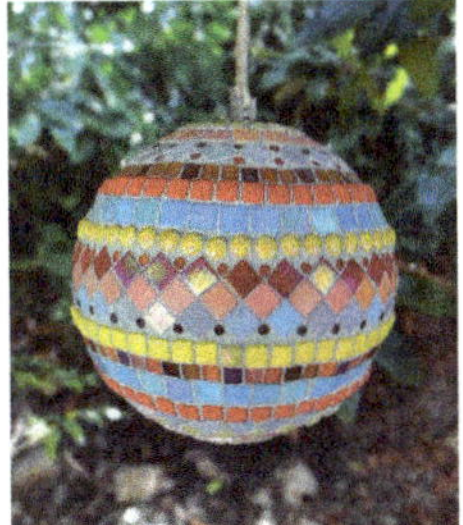

Mosaic Sphere no.1

The sphere is made of ready-made squares, without having to cut them. The beauty of the sphere comes from a harmonious combination of colors and the unique pattern created by combining the shapes.

Materials:

Glue covered polystyrene sphere with a wooden spike through
Different sized and colored glass squares: red, orange, yellow, light blue
Small glass circles
Tile glue
Glue bowl
A wooden stick or spatula
A thin screwdriver or toothpick to clean excess glue
Crème-colored grout
Grout Gear: Mixing bowl, water, a wooden stick, rags, gloves

1 Place the tile glue-glued polystyrene sphere on a small stabilizing tool.

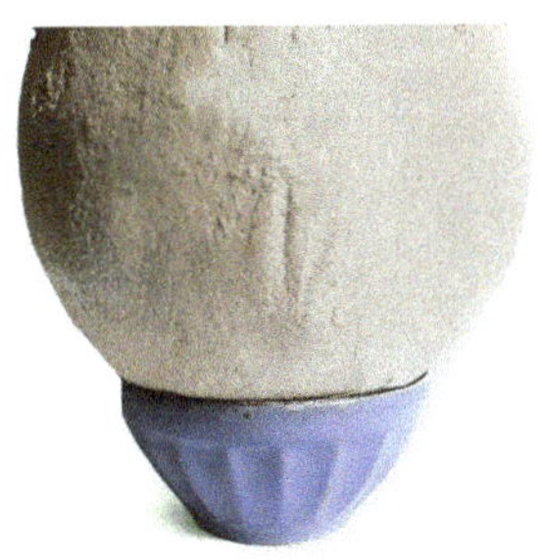

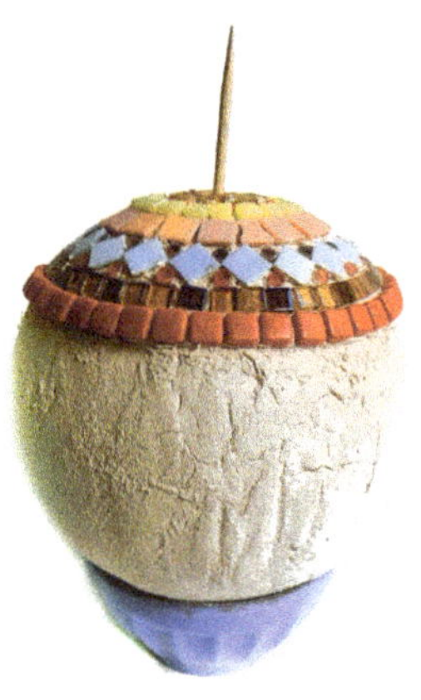

2 Start from the center of the sphere, around the spike. Glue squares and circles in a circular way, widening at each step, each line in a different color and size.

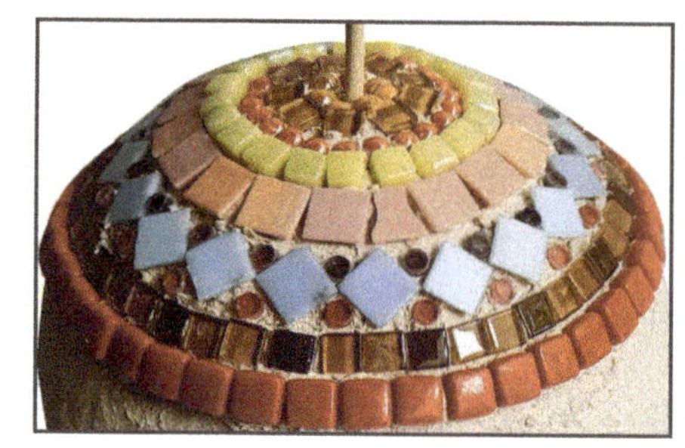

3 You should rotate the squares occasionally, and glue them as diamonds. You can glue small circles in the gaps created. Keep going that way until the sphere is fully covered. When reaching the center, flip the sphere 180° and glue colorful lines on the other side as well.

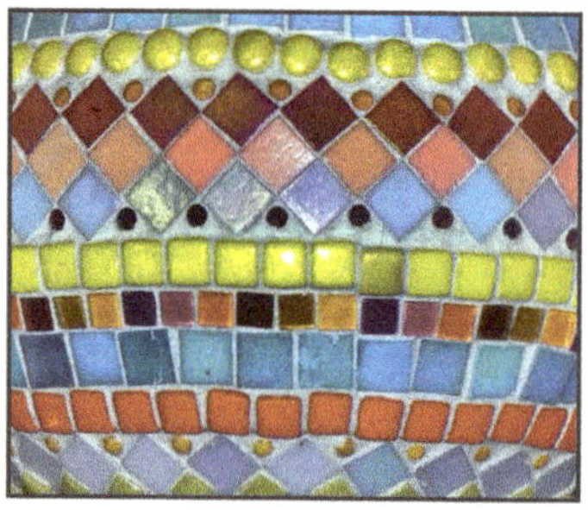

4 Wait a day for it to dry and fill with light-gray grout. Remove the spike and run a strong wire for hanging (see separate explanation).

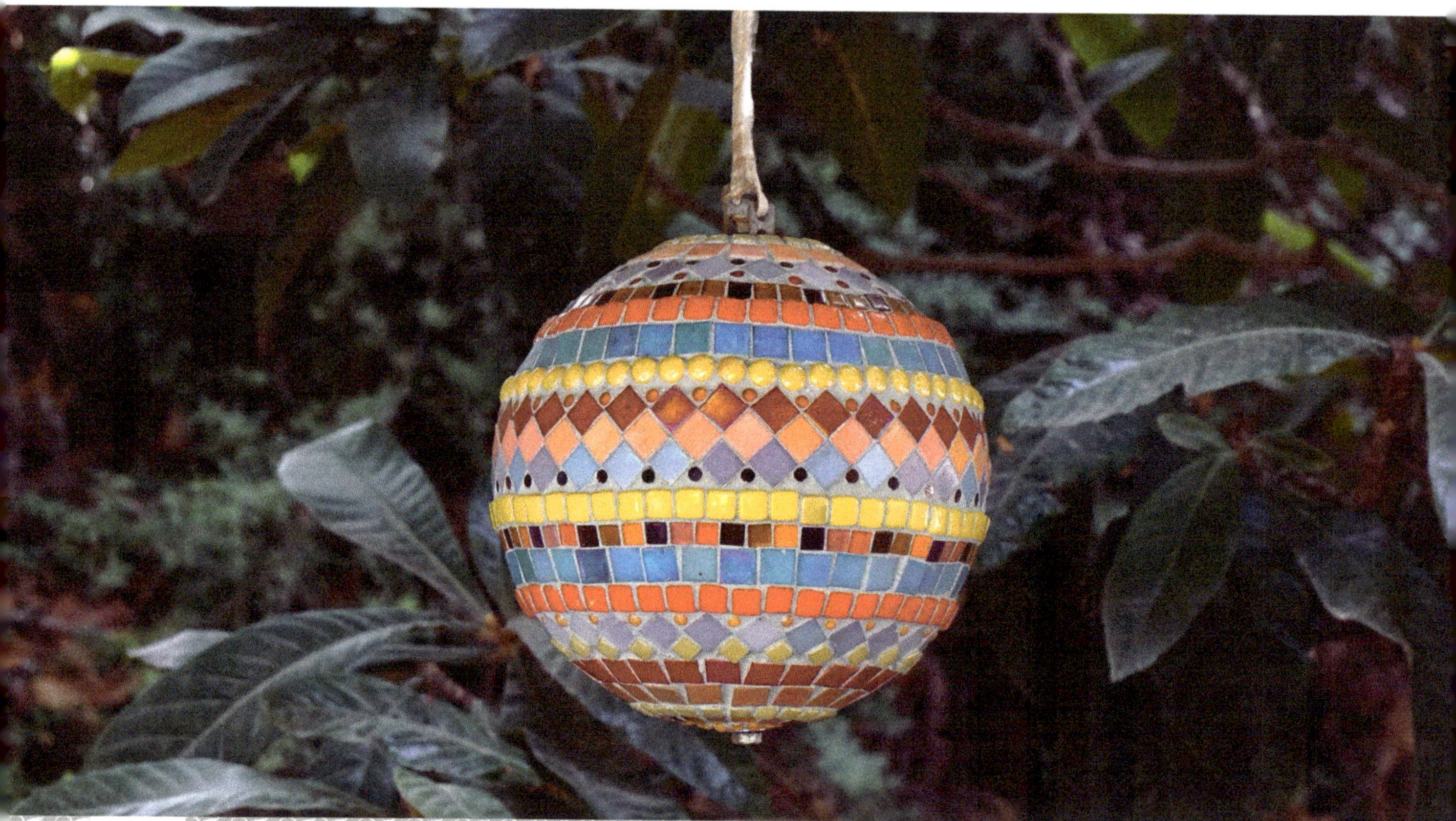

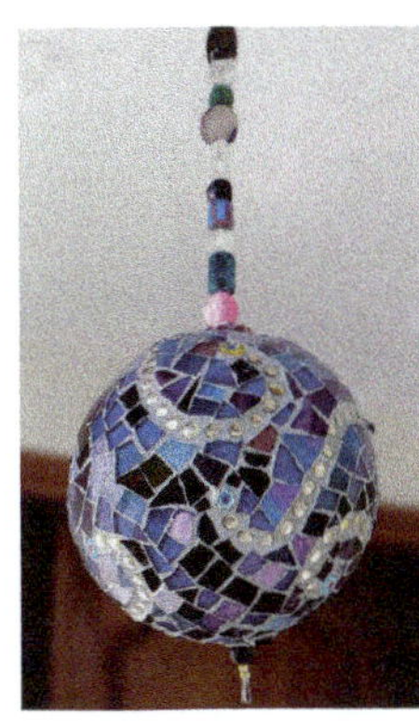

Mosaic Sphere no.2

A small mosaic sphere, combining purple glass and golden spirals. A simple pattern but the result is beautiful and glamorous.

Materials:

Glue covered polystyrene sphere with a wooden spike through
Golden small semi-circles
Small Millefiori circles
Purple glass
Wheeled glass nipper
Tile glue
Small glue bowl
A wooden stick or spatula
A thin screwdriver or toothpick
Gray grout
Grout Gear: Mixing bowl, water, a wooden stick, rags, gloves
Decoration beads
Strong nylon hanging wire (fishing line)

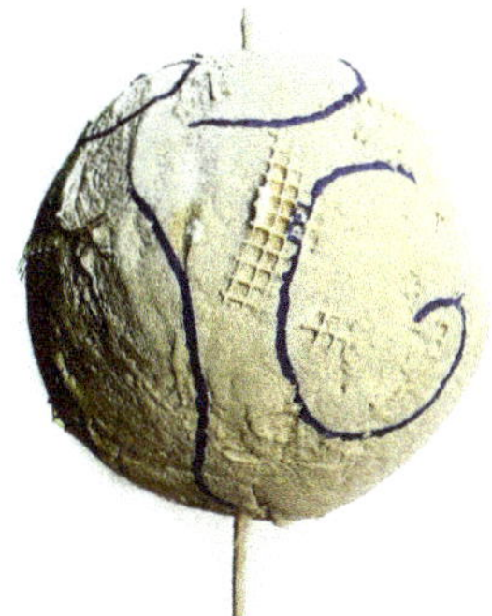

1 Using a marker, draw different spirals on the covered polystyrene sphere.

2 Start from the center of the sphere, around the spike. Glue squares and circles in a circular way, widening at each step, each line in a different color and size.

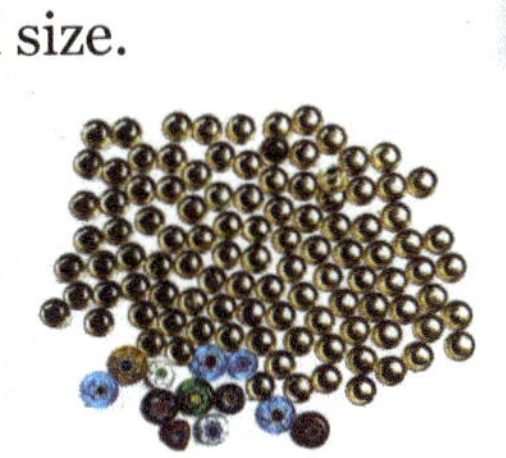

3 Using the wheeled nipper, cut purple glass into small pieces.

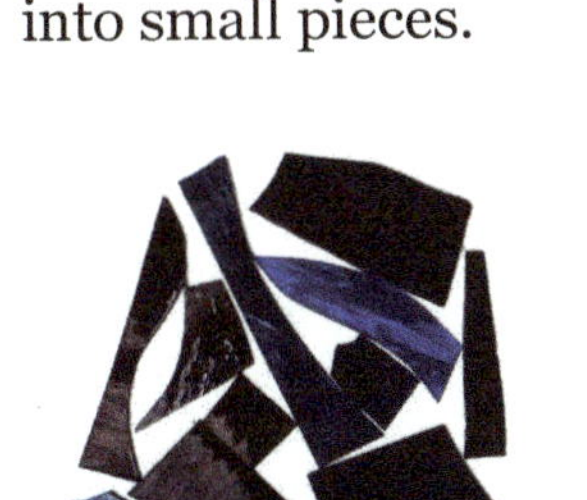

4 Glue the purple glass onto the sphere and wait a day for it to dry out. Prepare gray grout, clean, and polish the sphere with a wet rag or damp wipe. Remove the spike and thread a hanging wire. Decorate with beads and hang!

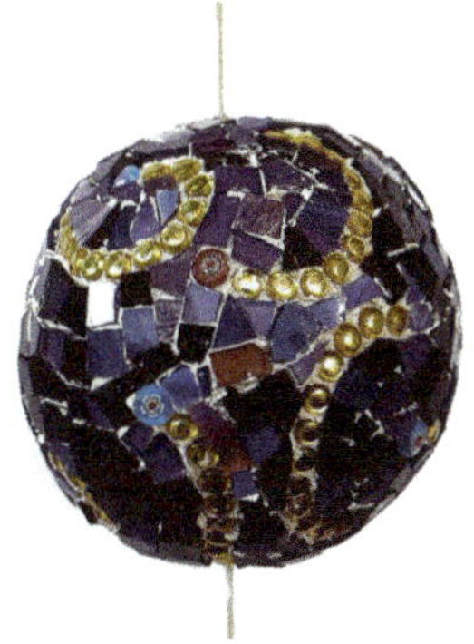

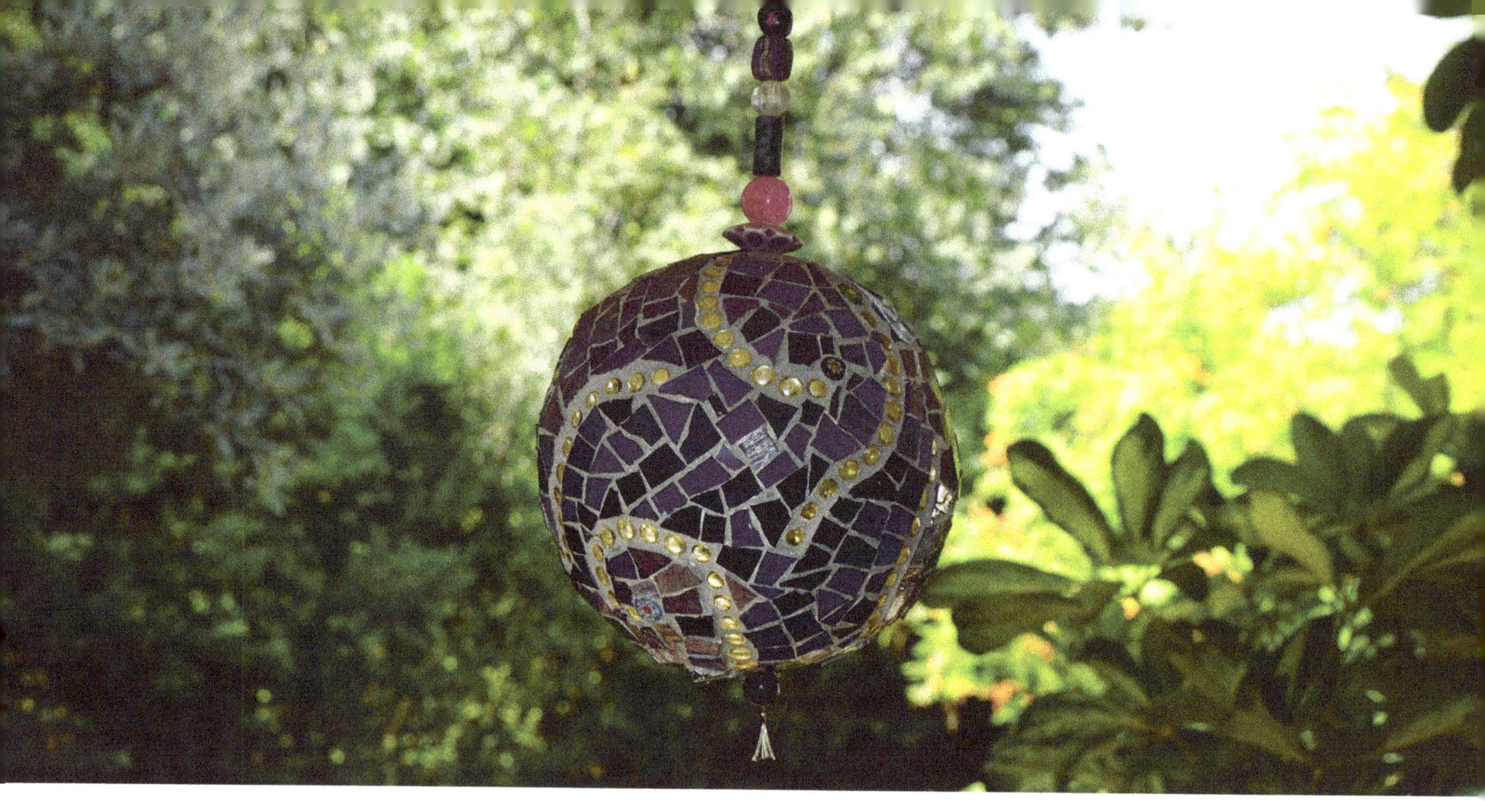

Using the Nipper to Cut Various Random Glass Shapes

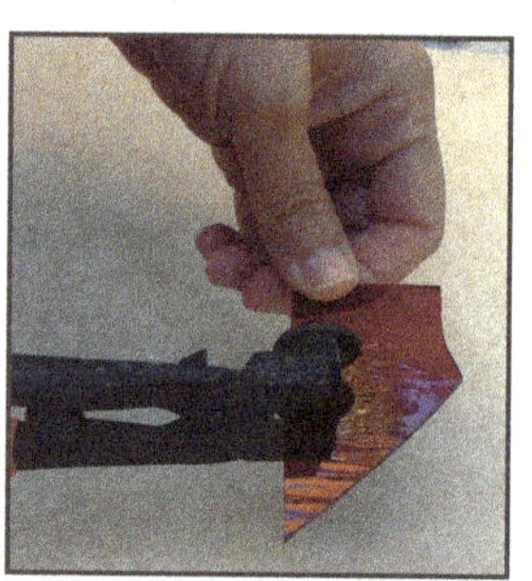

Before cutting, put on safety goggles to protect your eyes from small fragments.

Hold the glass nipper with your dominant hand by its bottom element. Use your other hand to hold the glass. Place the glass between the wheels and cut away. The shape you'll get depends on the angle and manner in which you hold the glass. Over time, you'll learn to control the nipper grip and succeed in creating whatever shape you like.

To cut (relatively) straight lines, it's important to hold the nipper at a straight angle to the glass.

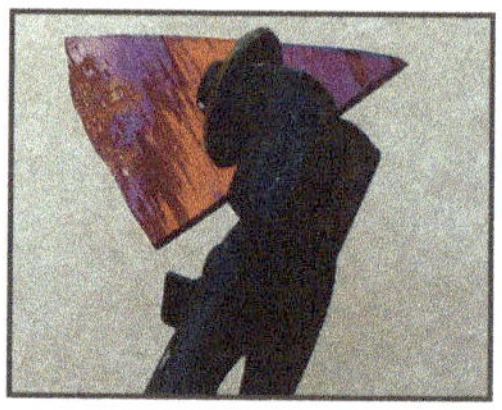

To cut a triangle shape, hold the nipper in an angle and cut to the desired shape.

Tip: When cutting glass, small pieces might ricochet. It is recommended to cut it into a wide and tall bowl (or even a plastic box). You should use gloves while cutting as to avoid any cuts and bruises.

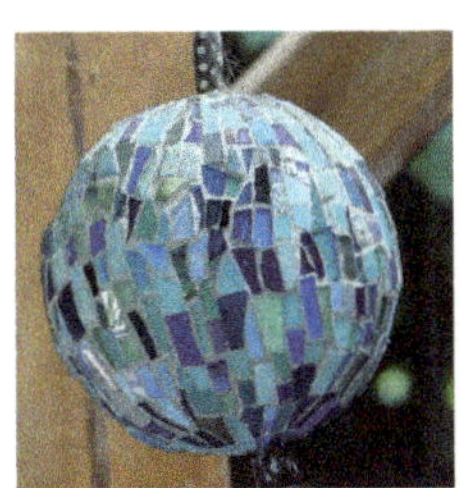

Mosaic Sphere no.3

A mosaic sphere made of blue and light blue glass stripes.

Materials:

Glue covered polystyrene sphere with a wooden spike through
Blue and light blue glass squares
Blue and light blue glass
Wheeled glass nipper
Tile glue
Small glue bowl
A wooden stick or spatula
A thin screwdriver or toothpick
Gray grout
Grout Gear: Mixing bowl, water, a wooden stick, rags, gloves
Decoration beads
Strong nylon hanging wire (fishing line)

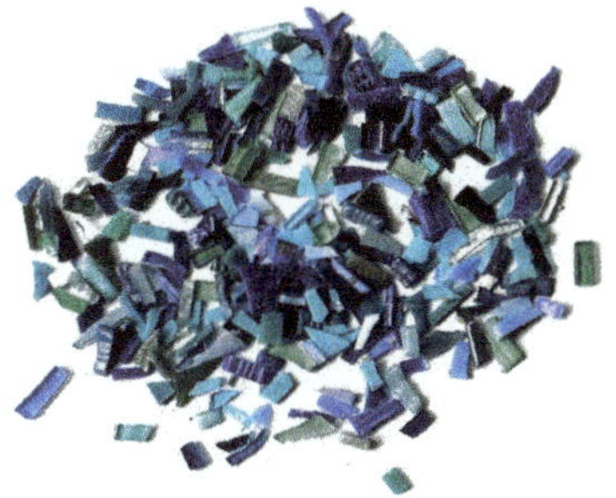

1 Prepare blue and light blue glass strips from glass squares or surfaces. The strips don't have to be the same width or length but should be narrow. Cut a few triangles as well – they will come handy where the ball gets narrower or wider.

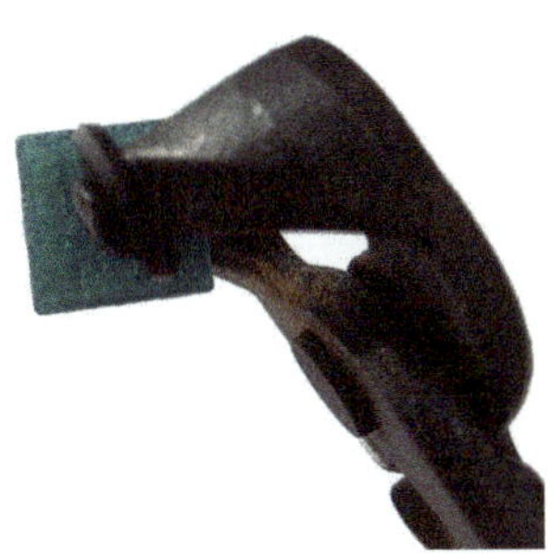

2 Use the wheeled nipper for cutting the glass squares. Hold the device with your dominant hand and grab the square by its center. Notice the angle of the device compared to the square; the way you'll hold it will determine the angle of the cut, straight or diagonal.

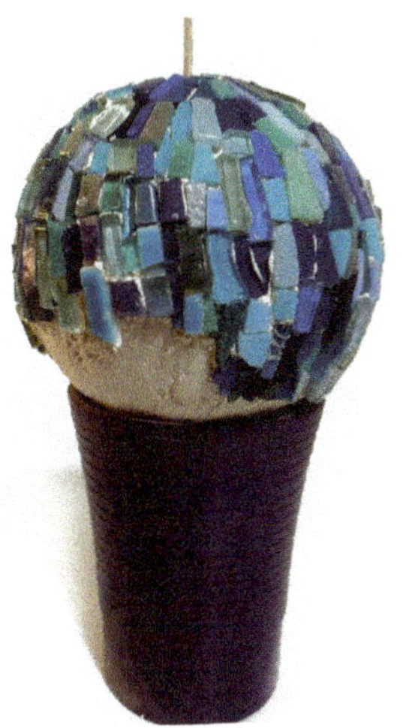

3 Place the sphere on a tall bowl and start gluing the strips from top to bottom. The cut triangles can be used to complete those spaces where a straight piece won't fit.

4 Flip the sphere around and keep gluing on the other side as well. You should maintain a nice finish around the hole.

5 Wait a day for it to dry and make gray grout, according to the instructions.

6 Thread the wire along the sphere and colorful beads to it. It's important to leave a hanging noose at the top of the wire.

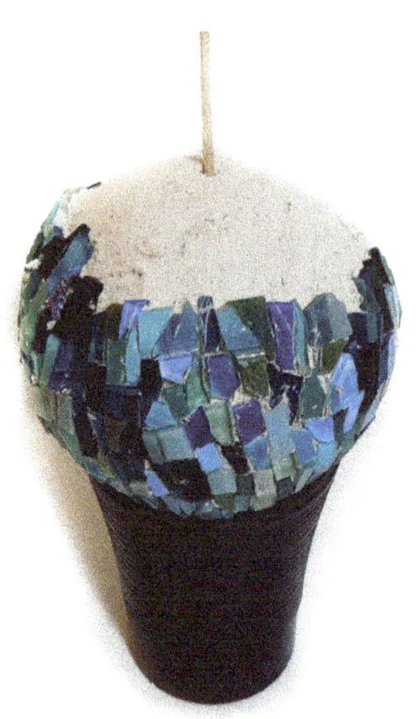

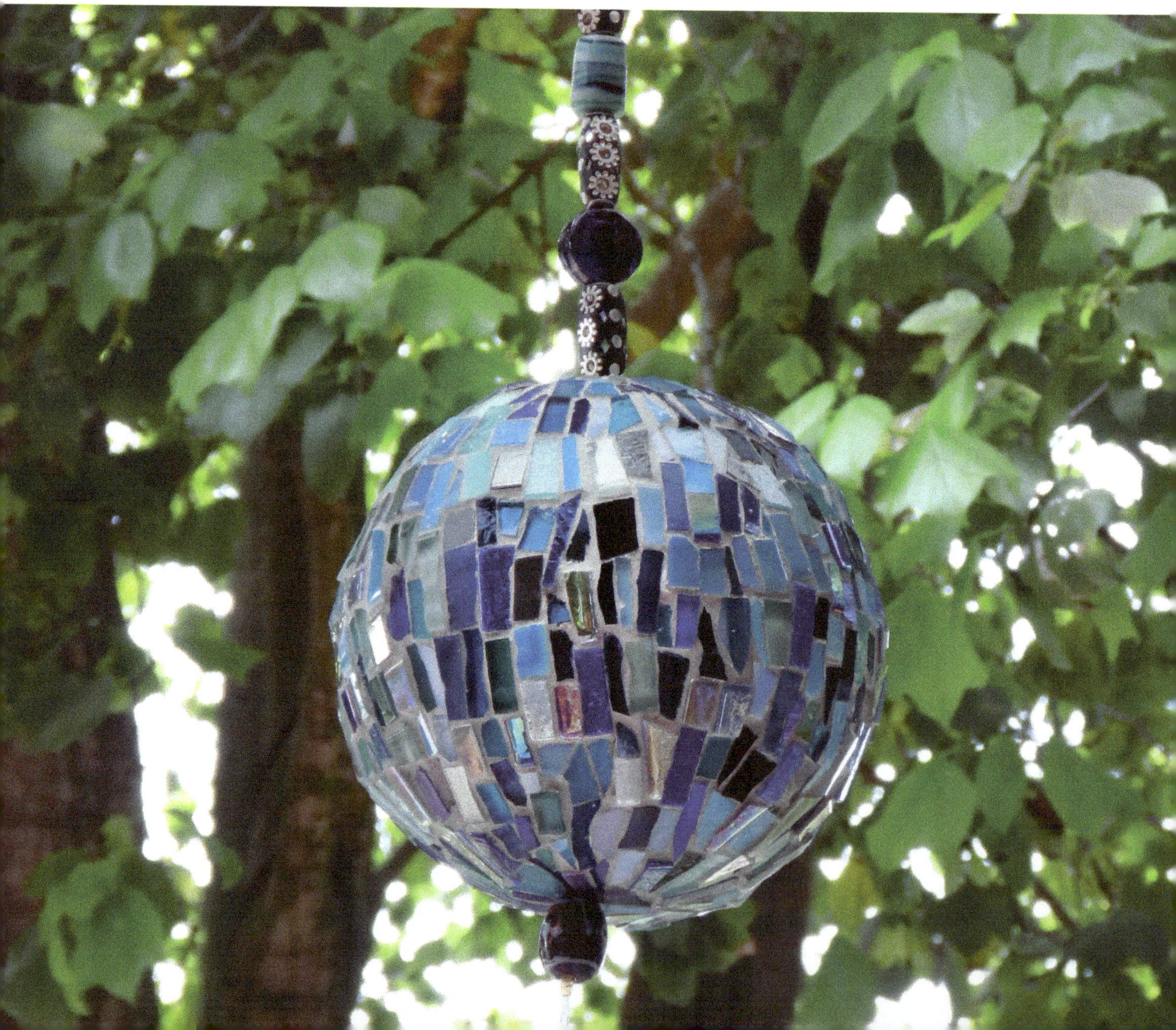

Cutting Glass into Strips

The technique for cutting glass is different than with ceramics. Here, we score the glass with a blade, then separate the two pieces.

Stained glass and mosaic artist use these glass cutting techniques, and to achieve maximum accuracy, each piece is machine-sanded after cutting. In this book, we'll only be using the blade and nipper.

There are several types of blades and hand grips. It's recommended that you use a quality cutter to make prolonged work more comfortable.

In order to cut accurate glass strips, use the cutting blade, L-square and pliers. First, we'll learn how to use the cutter.

For this purpose, you will need: a good glass knife, wooden L-square and a Breaking glass plier.

Steps of glass cutting - straight line:

* It is recommended to practice on clear and simple glass

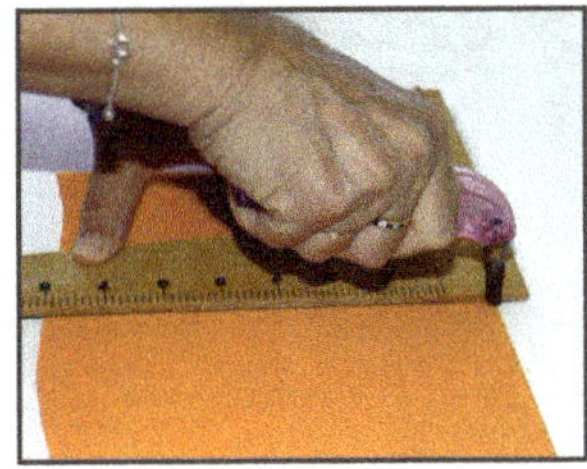

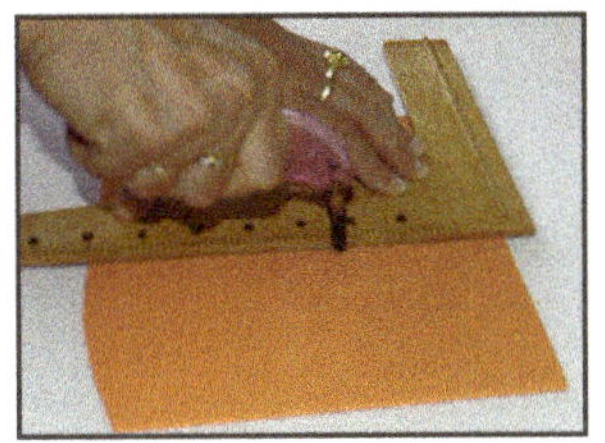

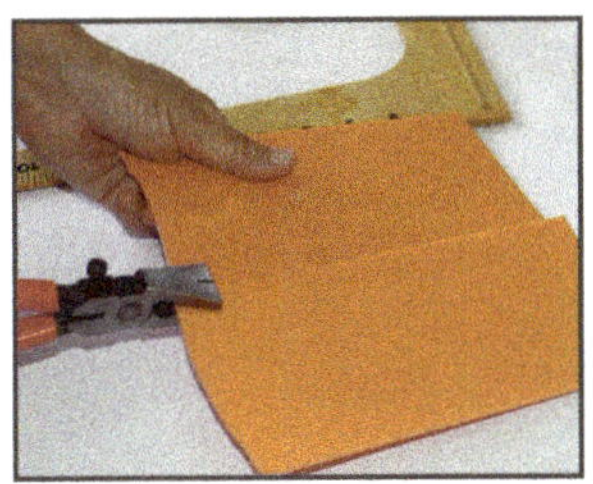

1. Place the panel you want to cut on a clean, level surface.
2. In order to cut a straight, accurate line, use a framing square or T-square: Place the square on the line you wish to cut.
3. Hold the glass cutter with your dominant hand and dip it in oil if necessary (required with certain types of cutters).
4. Place the cutter at the top or bottom edge of the glass and hold it straight, perpendicular to the glass.
5. Score the glass lengthwise with your dominant hand, while pressing on the square with your other hand to keep it in place. You can cut either from top to bottom or vice-versa. It's essential to do this while maintaining even pressure from edge to edge, otherwise the cut might become crooked. If you hear a slight ripping sound, you're doing it right.
6. Grab the glass by its bottom with running plier and snap it off. Note that the markings in the pliers are facing upward. The glass will snap in two along the line.

Cutting Glass into Strips by Size:

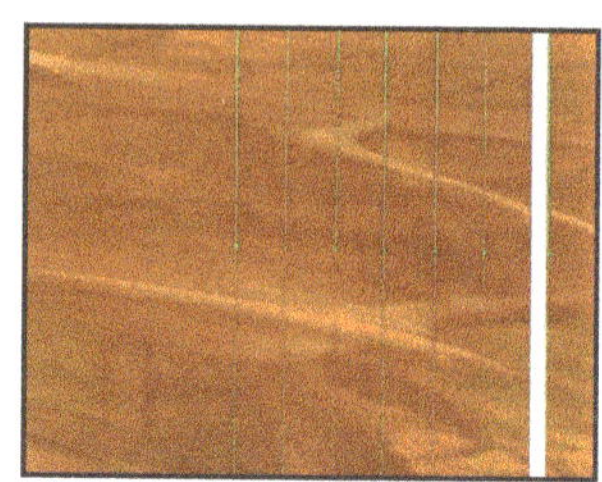

1. Place the glass you wish to cut on a clean, level surface.
2. Using a glass marker and T-square, mark the width you want to cut. You can mark all the desired lines in advance.
3. Place the T-square on the glass. Begin cutting the strips in order as explained before. Leave the wide part of the glass for last. Repeat stages 3-6 of glass cutting.

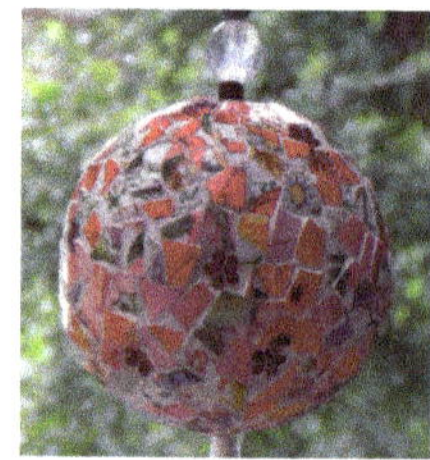

Mosaic Sphere no.4

A mosaic sphere made entirely out of colorful cup shards. The cups have patterns and decorations that are hard to find on tiles. Look for those you like and have a special color, pattern, or picture. Break the cups into little pieces to get a colorful surface.

Materials:

Glue covered polystyrene sphere with a wooden spike through
Colorful cups with patterns and textures
Beads or flowers for decoration
Wheeled glass nipper
Tile glue
Small glue bowl
A wooden stick or spatula
A thin screwdriver or toothpick
Crème grout
Grout Gear: Mixing bowl, water, a wooden stick, rags, gloves
Decoration beads
Strong nylon hanging wire (fishing line)

1 Cut the chosen cups into small random pieces using the nipper. It's important that the pieces will be small, so they won't stick out too much.

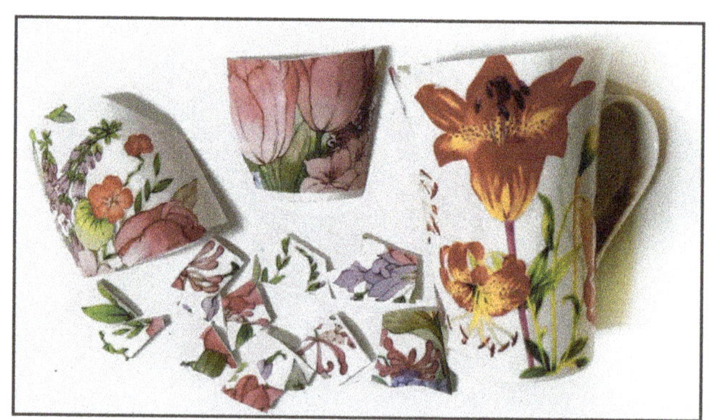

2 Place the sphere on a bowl. Glue the cut pieces using tile glue, from top to bottom. You can combine the cup pieces and decorations, like flowers or beads in the right color. Flip the sphere as you reach the halfway point and complete the pasting.

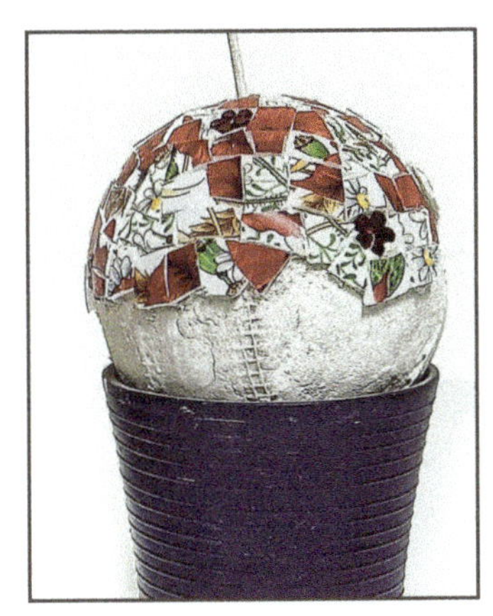

3 Wait for it to dry for a day and prepare the crème grout, according to the instructions.

4 Thread the wire and colorful beads to it. It's important to leave a hanging noose at the top of the wire.

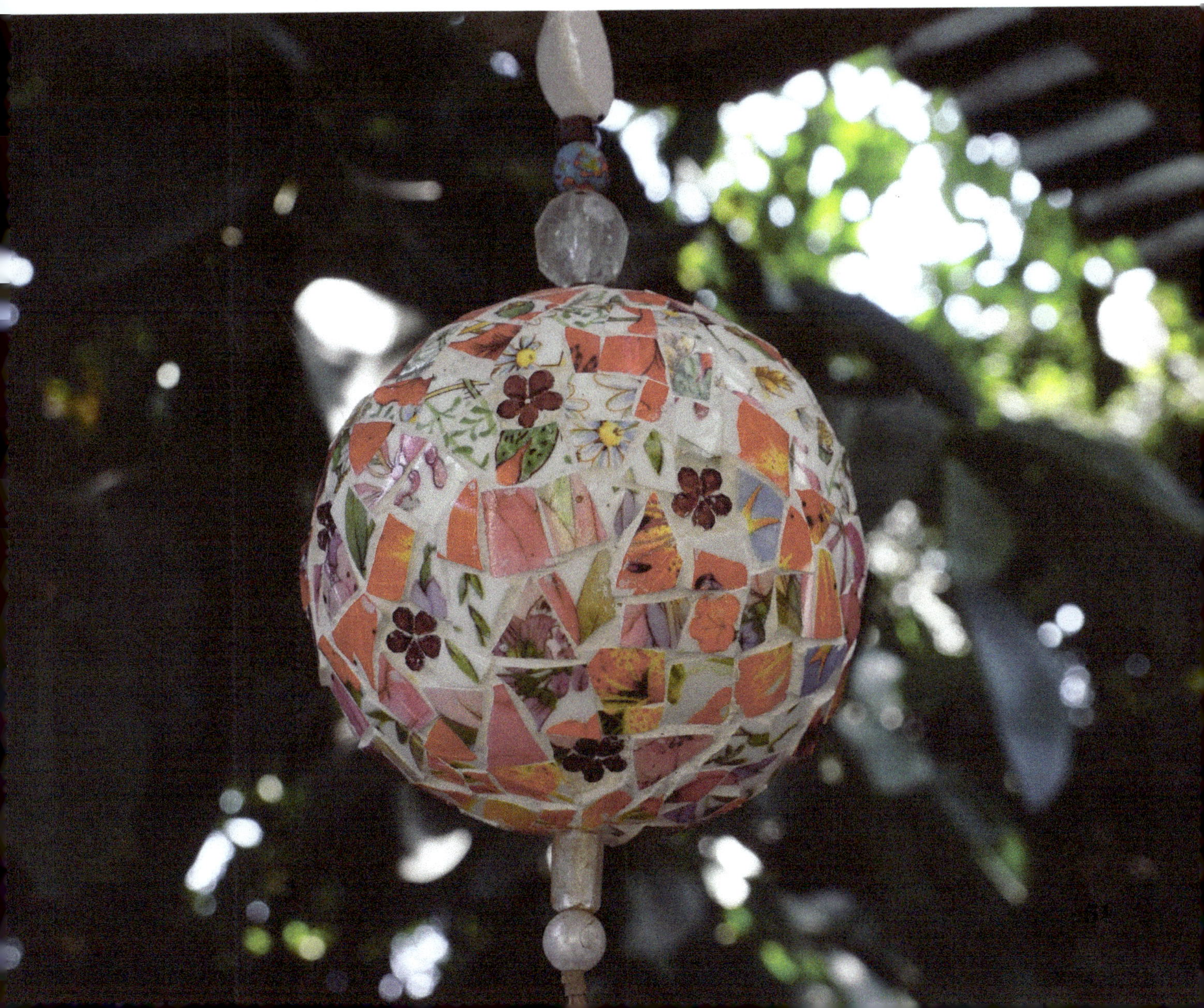

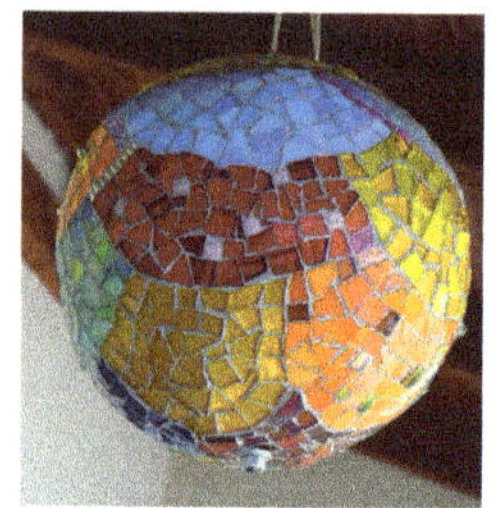

Mosaic Sphere no.5

A shiny and colorful mosaic sphere, a combination of cut glass and various beads. The sphere itself is made entirely out of arches and strips that surround one another. It looks different from every angle for the different material selection, which makes it unique.

Materials:

Glue covered polystyrene sphere with a wooden spike through
Glass sheets in several shades, light blue, yellow and red
Different kinds of flat beads in similar shades
Wheeled glass nipper
Tile glue
Small glue bowl
A wooden stick or spatula
A thin screwdriver or toothpick
Gray grout
Grout Gear: Mixing bowl, water, a wooden stick, rags, gloves

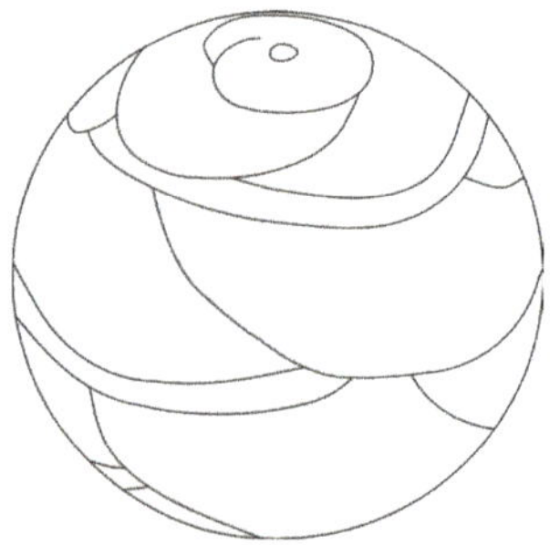

Pattern for the sphere:
Copy and enlarge according to the desire size.

1 Using a marker, draw the pattern on the sphere: start from a spiral at the top, around the spike, and continue by drawing arches around, some of them can be double (where the beads will go).

2 Start gluing from the top. First, create the first spiral, then add circles around it.

3 Glue lines of beads on the drawn strips and the arches – small pieces of cut glass. You can mix in shades of gray into the arches, but you should use similar colors as to have a harmonious colorful surface.

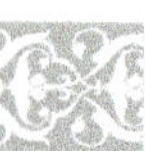

4 Glue a different color in each section. You should first border the area with beads and then fill the colorful arch with the colorful glass pieces you cut using the nipper.

5 Turn the sphere over and complete the pasting until you reach the bottom. Wait a day for it dry and prepare gray grout, according to the instructions.

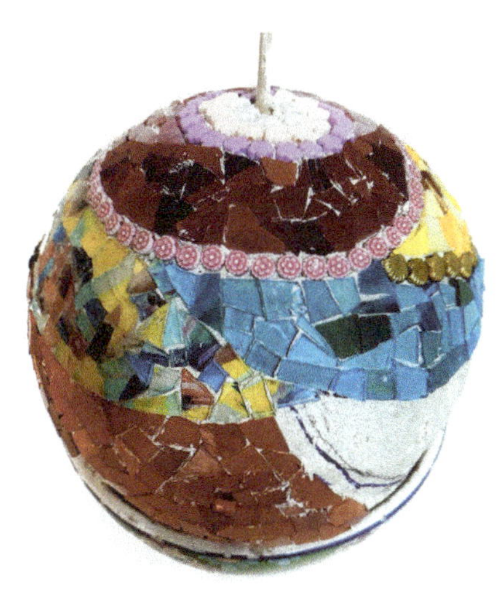

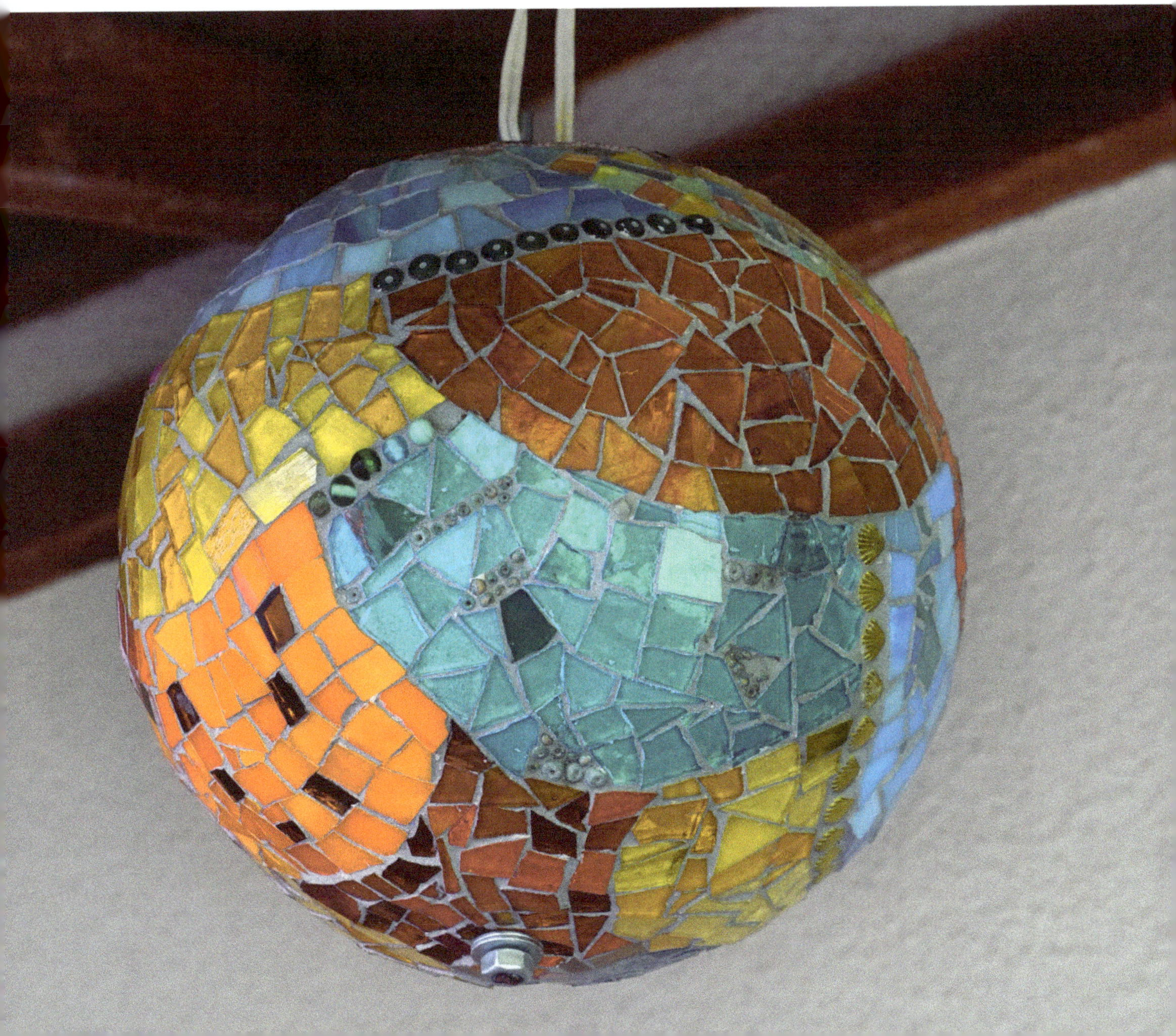

Suspending the Spheres

If the spheres are small, you can hang them with a fishing line or chain. In case they are heavy, a wire won't hold them, and you'd have to use a metal wire connected to a chain or a stronger kind of wire.

Using a fishing line to hang small spheres

1 Fold a fishing line in two. Hold on both its ends, thread a round bead and under it a thick metal clamping bead. Flatten the bead well with a nipper, that will serve as the stopping point for the wire and hold the sphere. You can alternatively tie a strong knot instead of the clamping bead.

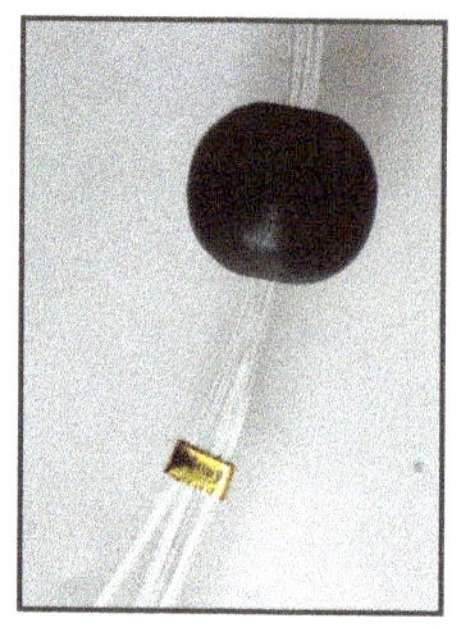

2 Pull out the spike and thread the wire instead, to the other side of the sphere, with the loop at the top part.

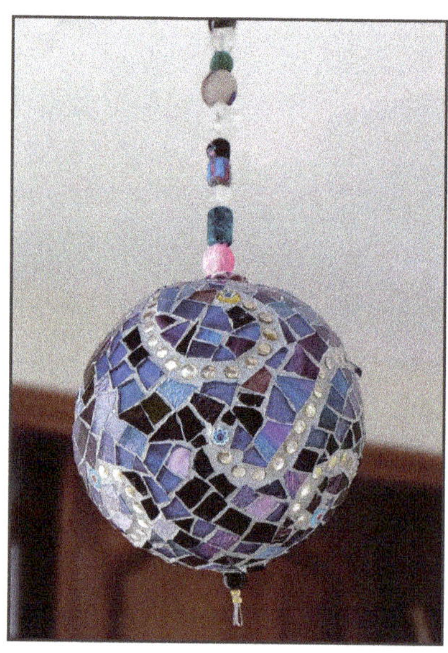

3 Thread beads from the top of the sphere, above the ball. Leave a hanging noose at the top part of the wire.

The sphere is now ready to be hung on a nail or tree branch.

Hanging a Heavy Sphere

1 Pull out the wooden spike and thread a long metal screwing rod instead.

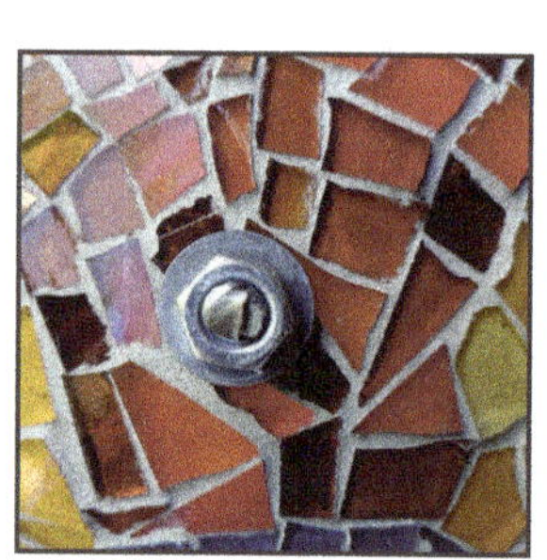

2 Seal the bottom part of the sphere with a lug nut and tighten well. This will be the hanging base and it should be strong and not fall apart.

3 Thread a metal angle with two holes at the top of the pole and screw a lug nut above it. You should cut the pole in the right length, so it doesn't stick over the sphere.

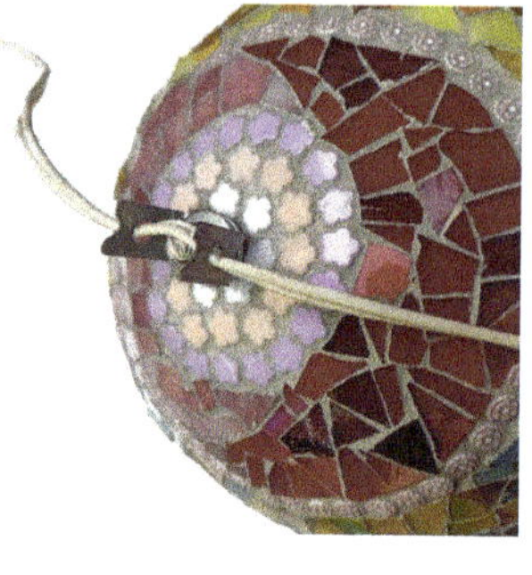

4 Thread a wire and use it to hang the sphere (electric wire, chain or a rope that can hold it).

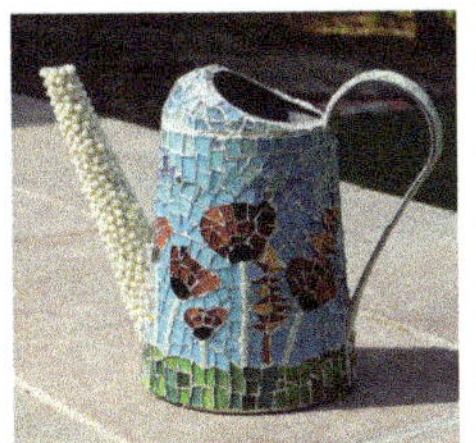

Project: Decorative Metal Funnel

If you make mosaics, you know you should open your eyes and look around, perhaps you'll stumble upon great findings that will be great for coating, pasting or reconstruction. Once, when my neighbor threw away a metal funnel, it seemed great to me for some mosaic work. Red flowers on the backdrop of pearl beads did the job, and you can see the results here. I can even keep using it to water the plants... practical and a great garden ornament.

Materials:

A metal funnel (not plastic)
Glass in shades of black, green, light blue, red and orange
Small green beads for the stocks
Flat white pearl-like beads
Glass squares in light blue and green shades
Tweezers
Tile glue
Small glue bowl
A wooden stick or spatula
A thin screwdriver or toothpick
Crème grout
Grout Gear: Mixing bowl, water, a wooden stick, rags, gloves

1 Prepare the funnel for pasting: clean from dust and make sure it's smooth.

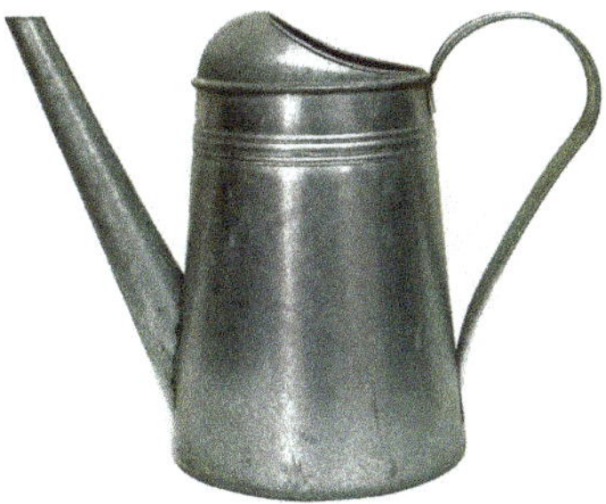

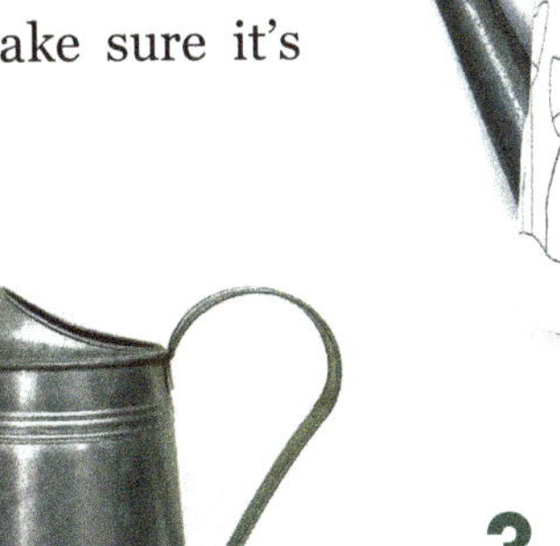

2 Print out the pattern and copy it onto the funnel using a copying paper.

3 Trace the pattern with a marker.

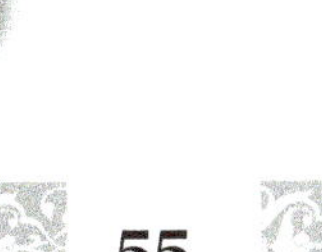

4 Start from the center of the flowers – cut the center of each from black glass, in one piece. You can start from semi-circles and adjust the shape.

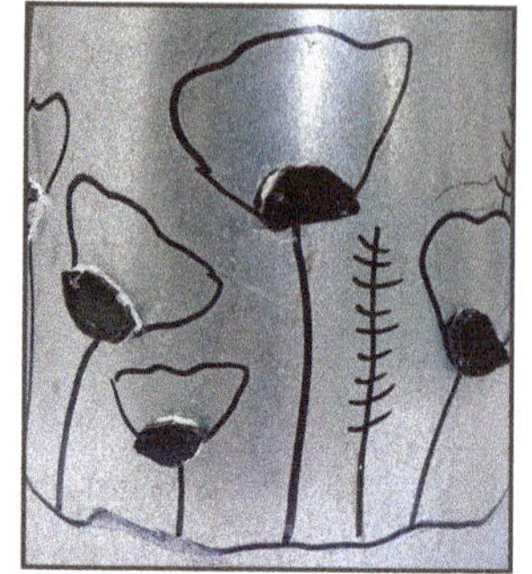

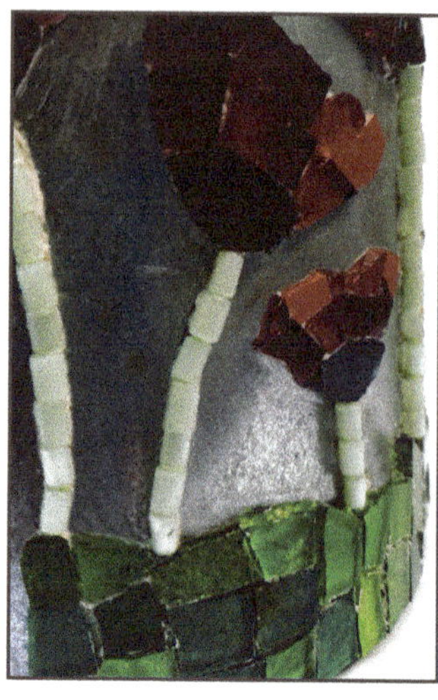

5 Cut red glass into small shapes and complete the flowers.

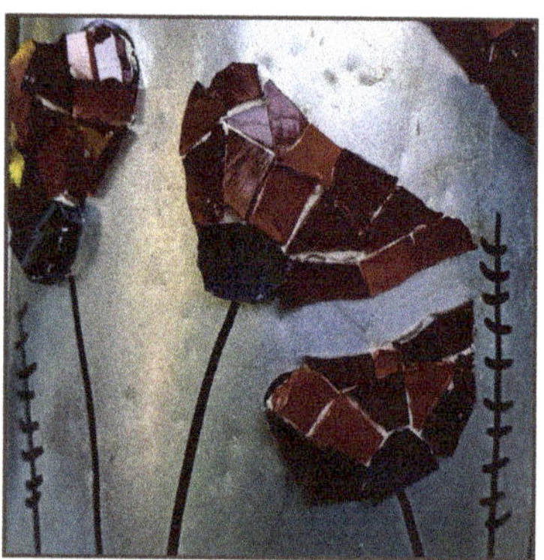

6 Add elongated beaded stocks and grass out of green glass, cut into little pieces.

7 Cut out long and thin triangles out of yellow/orange glass and complete the thorns between the flowers. You can cut the triangles from a long stripe of glass, like the sample shows.

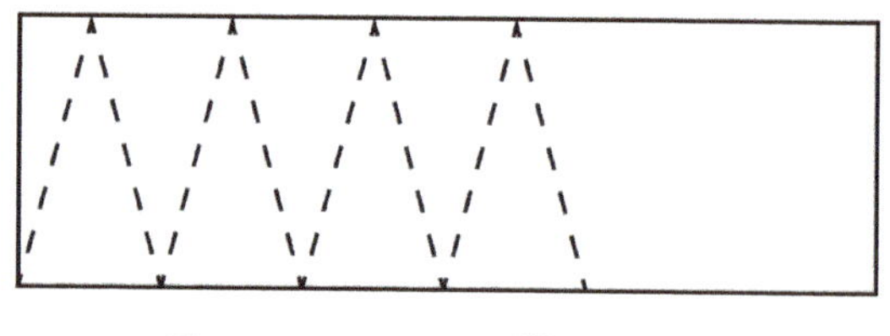

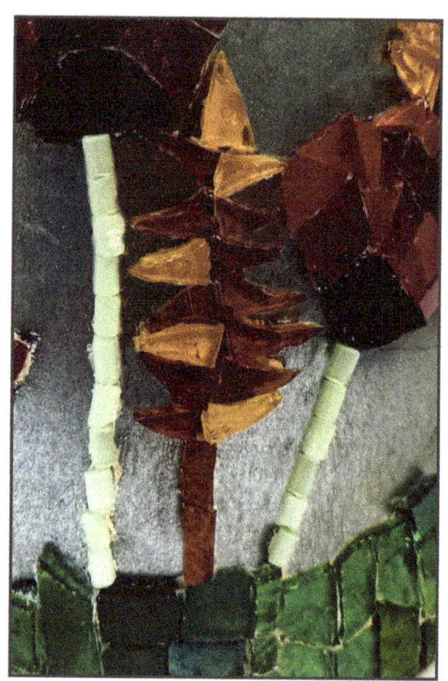

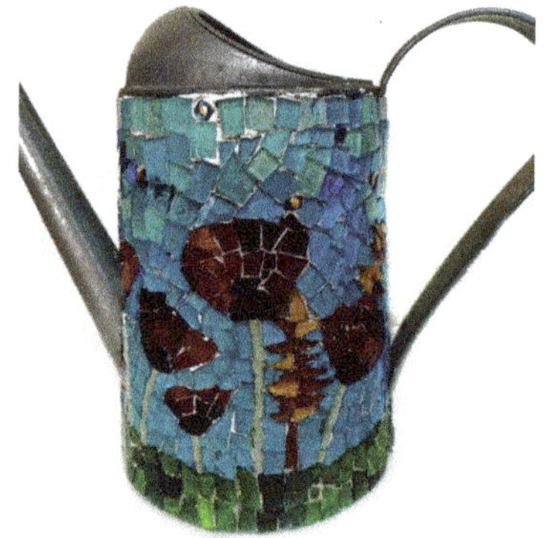

8 Cut out light blue glass into random pieces and complete the background. You can also incorporate nuggets or same sized glass beads.

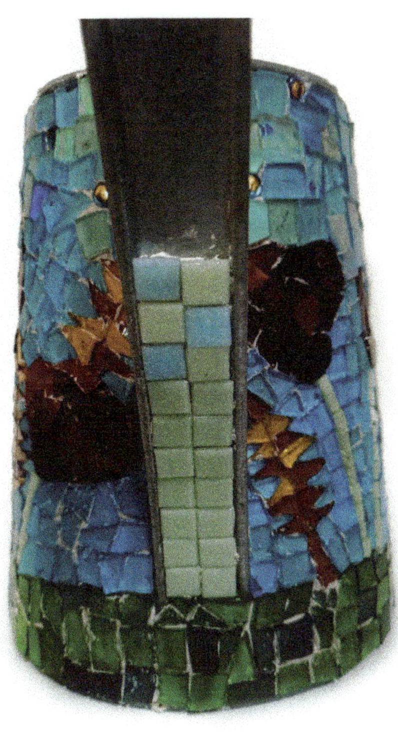

9 Glue green and light blue squares on the funnel's handle, to fit the width of the handle.

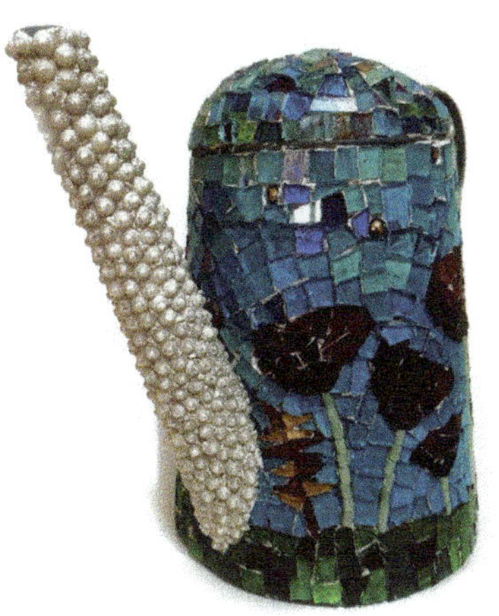

10 Glue white, flat beads on the funnel's nozzle, it will give it a fancy look. In case the beads are rugged, you should leave the nozzle without grout and make sure the tile glue fills up the spaces.

11 Once the funnel is dry, you can apply light grout, according to the instructions, clean and polish it.

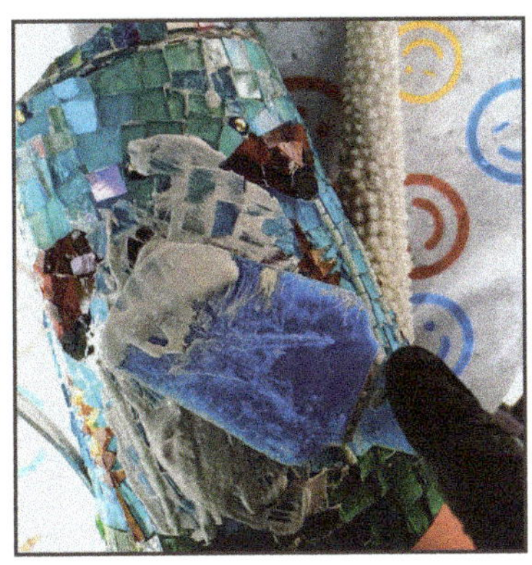

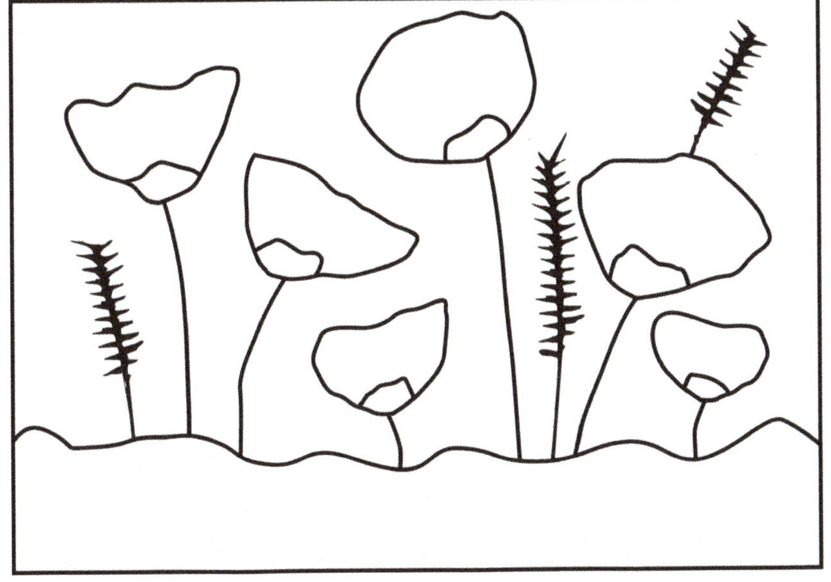

Pattern for the funnel:
Copy and enlarge according to the desire size.

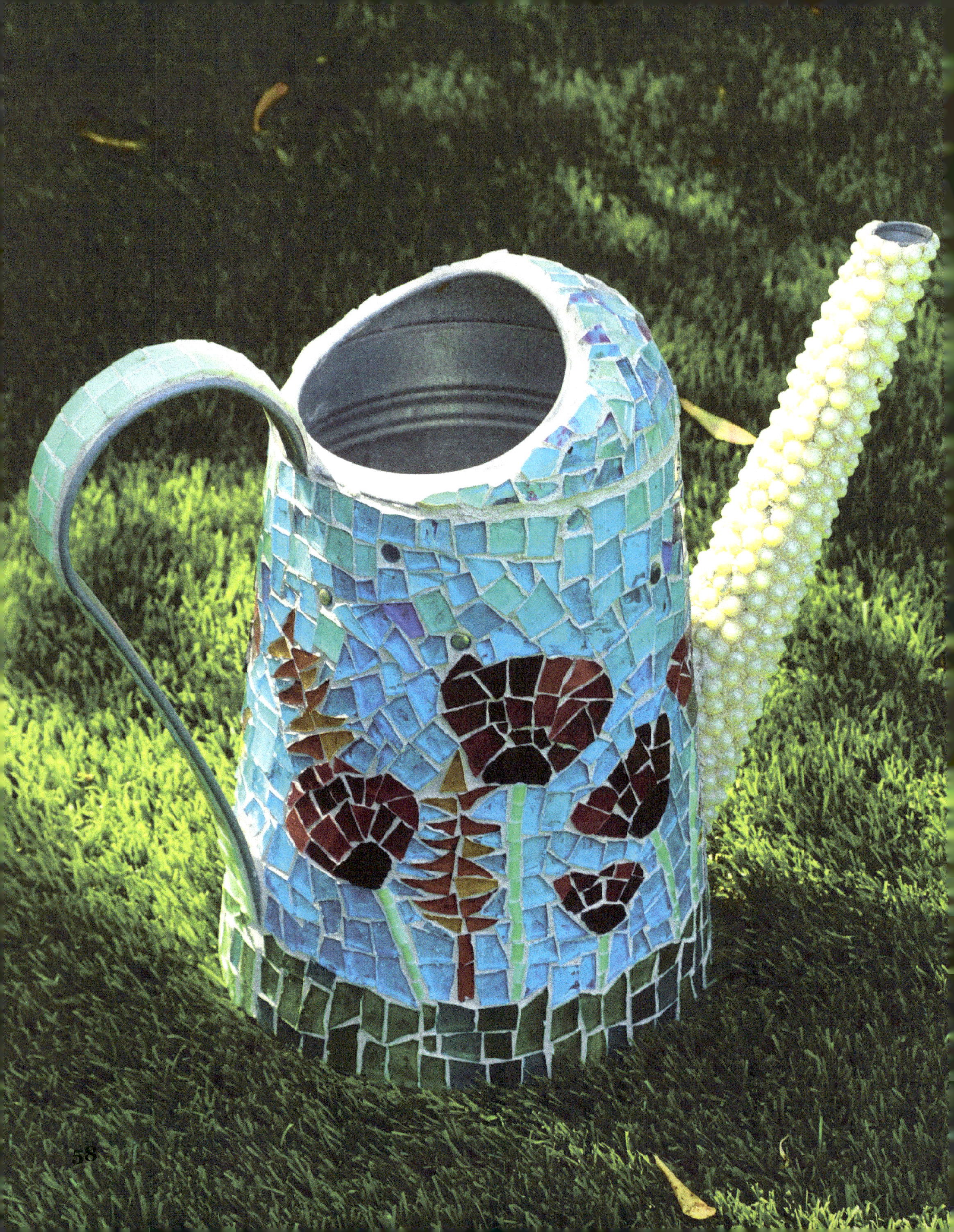

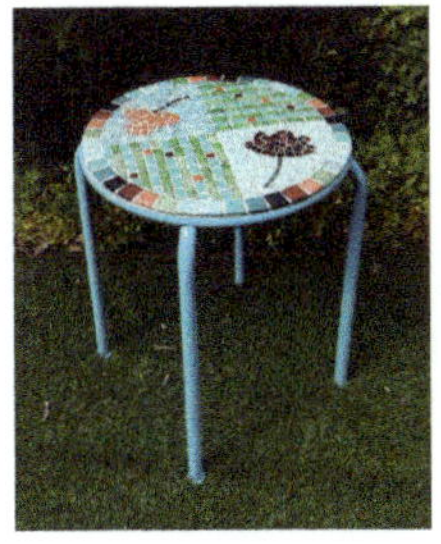

Project: Light Blue Round Table

Metal tables can be found in various shades (and painted too). I loved the light blue shade of that table, and the pattern matches its shades. It's a relatively small table but you can match the pattern to any size table you'd like. In this pattern we used glass squares, the kind you can buy in sheets or by the pound, in a few ways and cutting techniques – some are whole, some cut in half, some random or small strips.

A color combination is harmonious and pleasing to the eye, incorporating matte with shiny colors, which makes it even more interesting. You can switch them for ceramic squares or change the color scheme accordingly.

Materials:

A round metal table
Glass squares in shades of red (crimson), orange, light blue, green
A wheeled nipper
Tile glue
Small glue bowl
A wooden stick or spatula
A thin screwdriver or toothpick
Crème grout
Grout Gear: Mixing bowl, water, a wooden stick, rags, gloves

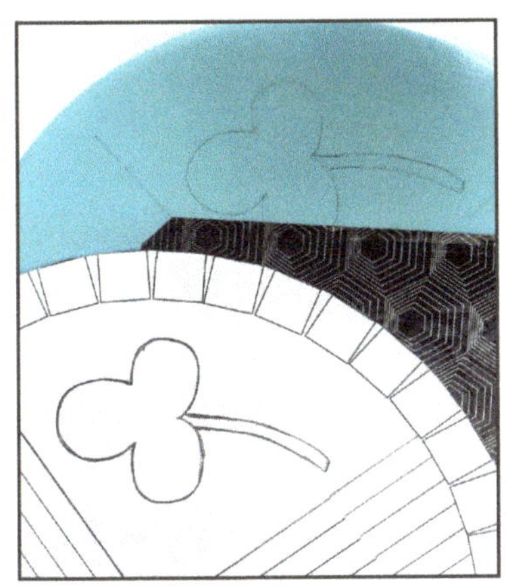

1 Print out the pattern at the desired size and copy it onto the table. Go over it with a marker, if needed.

2 Prepare squares according to the desired color scheme. Here I used black, crimson, orange, a few hues of blue and green.

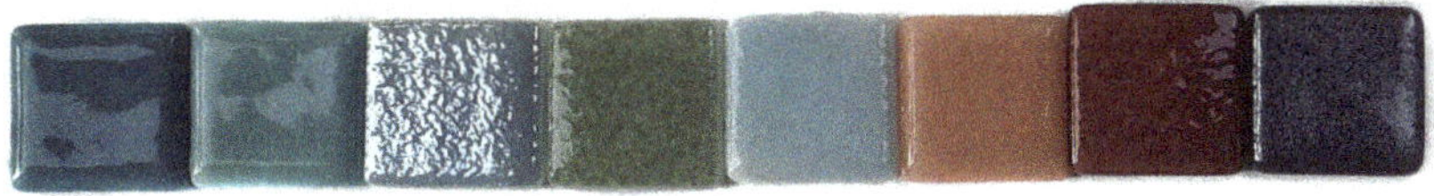

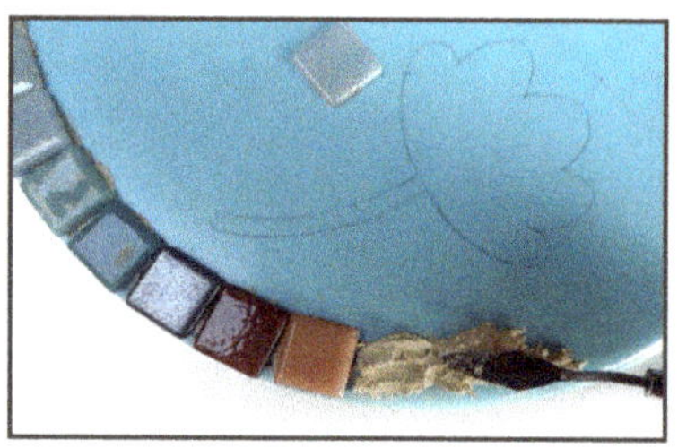

3 Start from the table frame – arrange the squares in the desired order; apply tile glue using the spatula and glue.

4 To make the first flower, cut orange tiles into random pieces and glue close together. It's important to make sure the edges are rounded to create the arch of the flower. Cut little black rectangles and glue the stock.

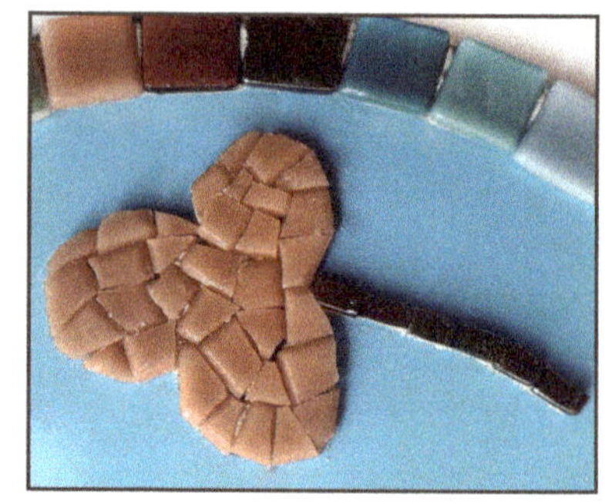

5 The second flower is made the same way, red instead of orange.

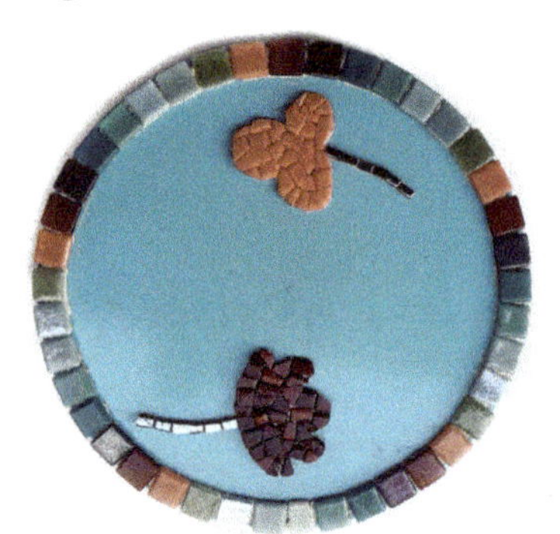

6 The background for the flowers completes a semi-circle: start from the frame and make sure to glue straight pieces close together along the line. Fill in the remaining area with pieces in different sizes. Here I used light blue, silver and sparkly.

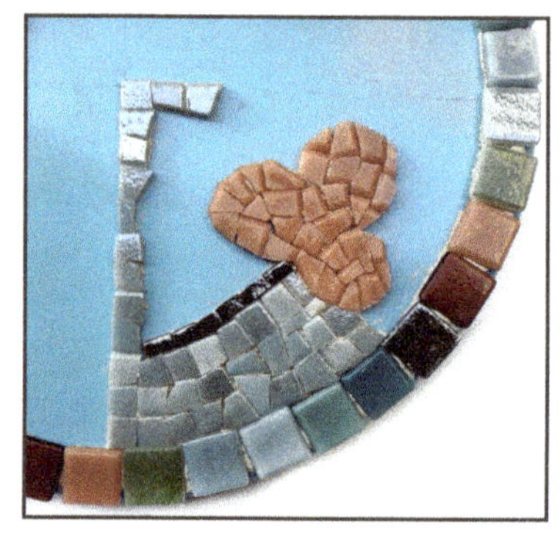

7 Complete the second quarter in the same manner, each with a different shade of light blue.

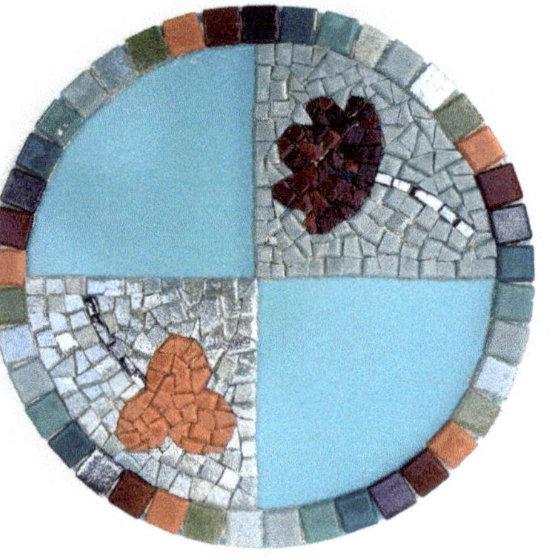

8 Using the wheeled nipper, cut glass squares in two shades of green into half. Prepare small squares in shades of orange and brown, at the strips' width to incorporate with the background strips.

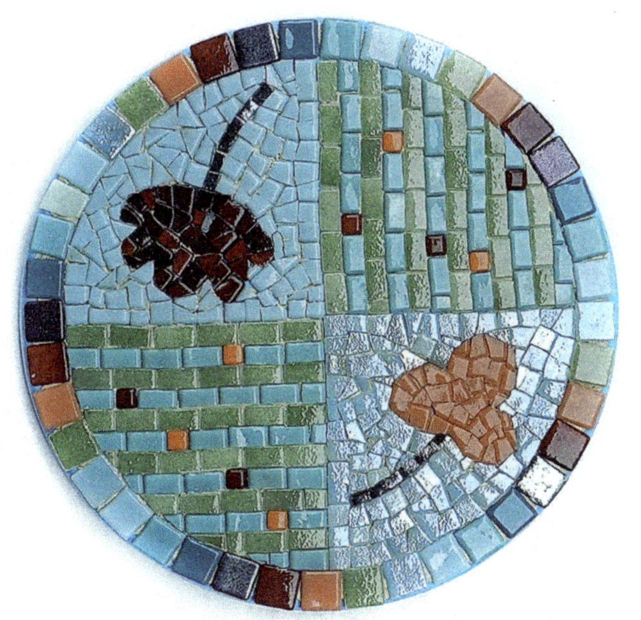

9 Fill out the background at the remaining quarters with green strips, and a few small squares in between. The strips should be at a different direction at every quarter.

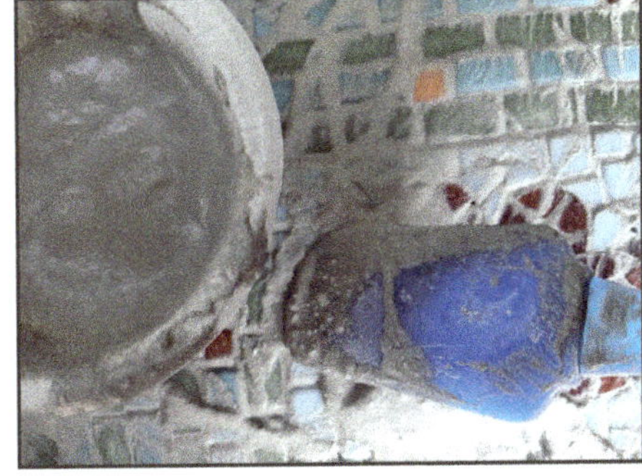

10 Wait a day for it to dry and make grout according to instructions. Clean and polish, and the table is done!

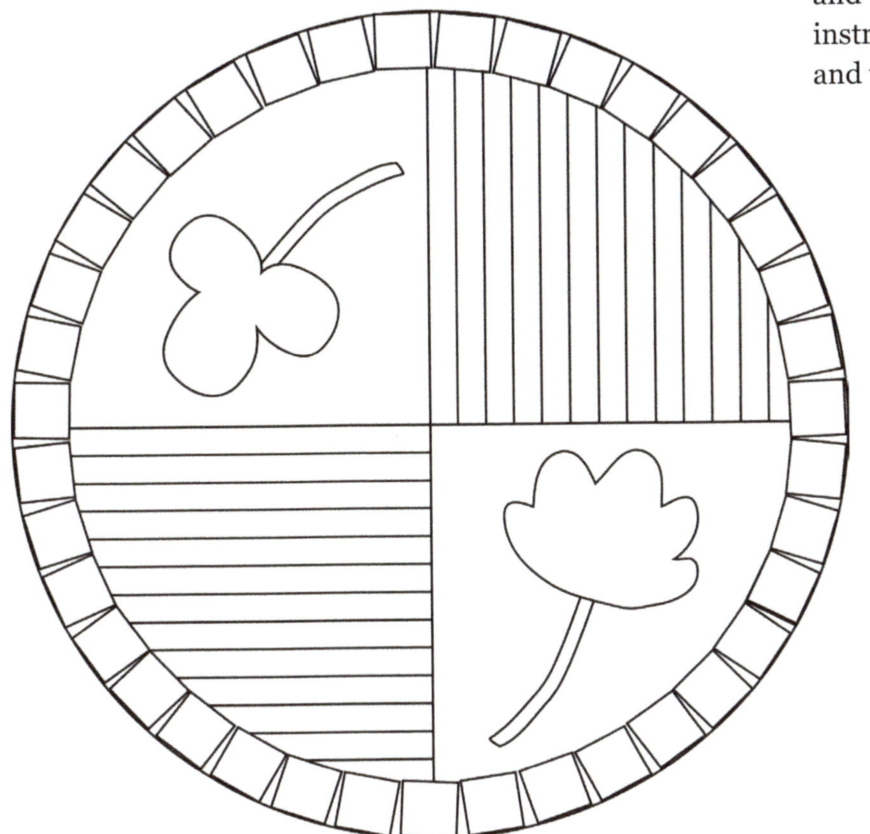

Pattern for the table:
Copy and enlarge according to the desire size.

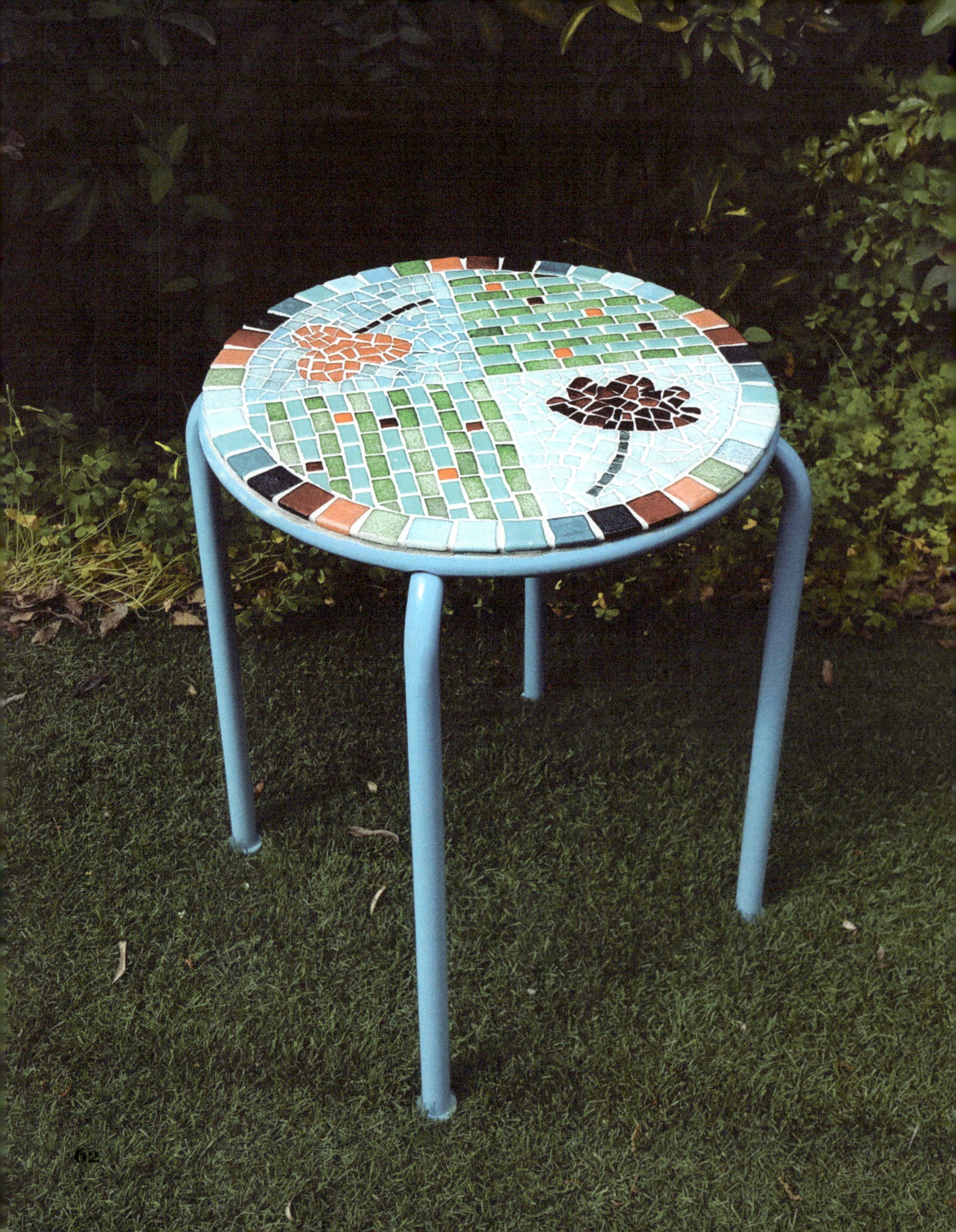

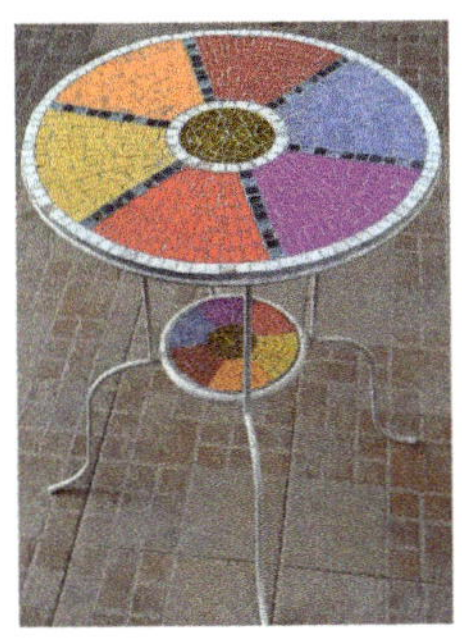

Project: Colorful Round Table

Every porch needs a small and nice table, enough for two people for their morning or afternoon coffee (or herbal tea, in my case). It's a simple pattern but you can make it in different colors and materials, and it will fit any sized round table. I used ceramics in shades of red, yellow, orange, brown, purple, and light blue. And in the center are gold squares, to give it a shiny element. The squares defining the table give it a straight and cohesive frame.

It's important to make sure all the materials you use are the same height, so you'd get a table as straight as possible.

Materials:

Round metal table
Ceramic tiles in 7 shades
Glass or stone squares as thick as the ceramics in shades of black and white
Ceramics cutting nipper
Tile glue
Small glue bowl
A wooden stick or spatula
A thin screwdriver or toothpick
Gray grout
Grout Gear: Mixing bowl, water, a wooden stick, rags, gloves

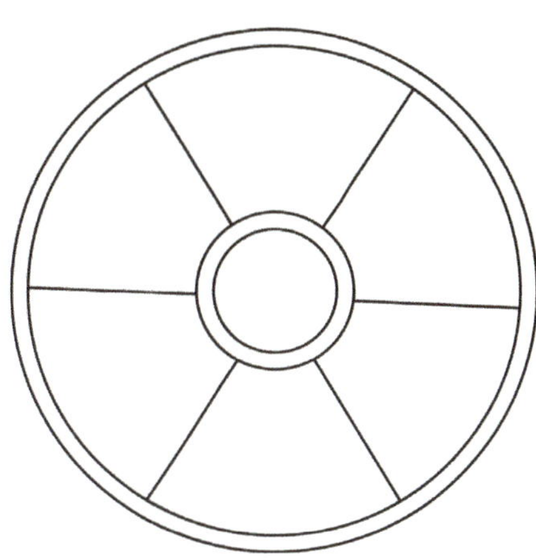

1 Print out the pattern in the left size and copy it onto the table or sketch it directly on (it's important to locate the small circle in the center).

2 Prepare your materials: white square for the border, black squares for separating the colors. Choose 7 shaded ceramics. It's important that all materials you choose will be at the same height.

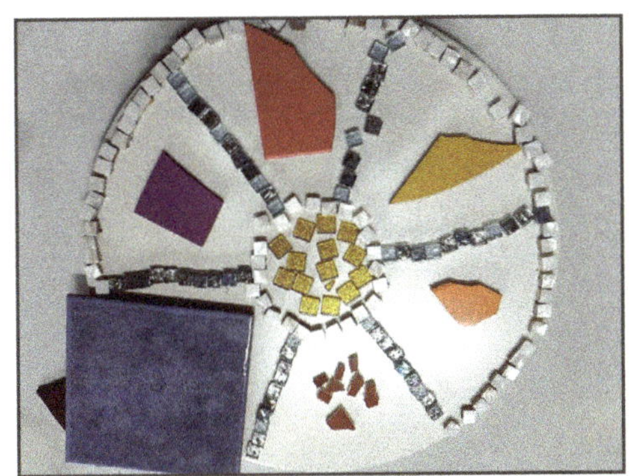

3 Start from the outline: first glue the white squares, to create both circles. Then, create the separation lines. It's important to clean the excess glue after gluing, so they don't dry out and get in the way later.

4 cut the ceramics you picked to different sized rectangles. You can cut strips with a cutting machine or use a combined nipper for cutting strips; it will make your job easier.

5 Glue strips of different colors in each part. Make sure to have as smooth edges as possible.

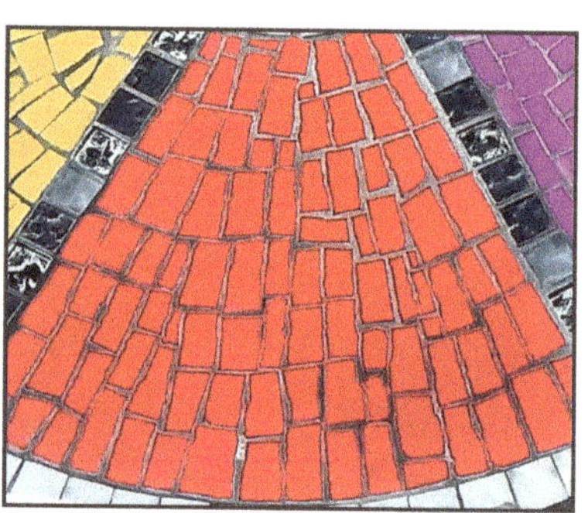

6 Wait for it dry for a day and fill in with gray grout, according to instructions. Clean well and shine with a damp wipe.

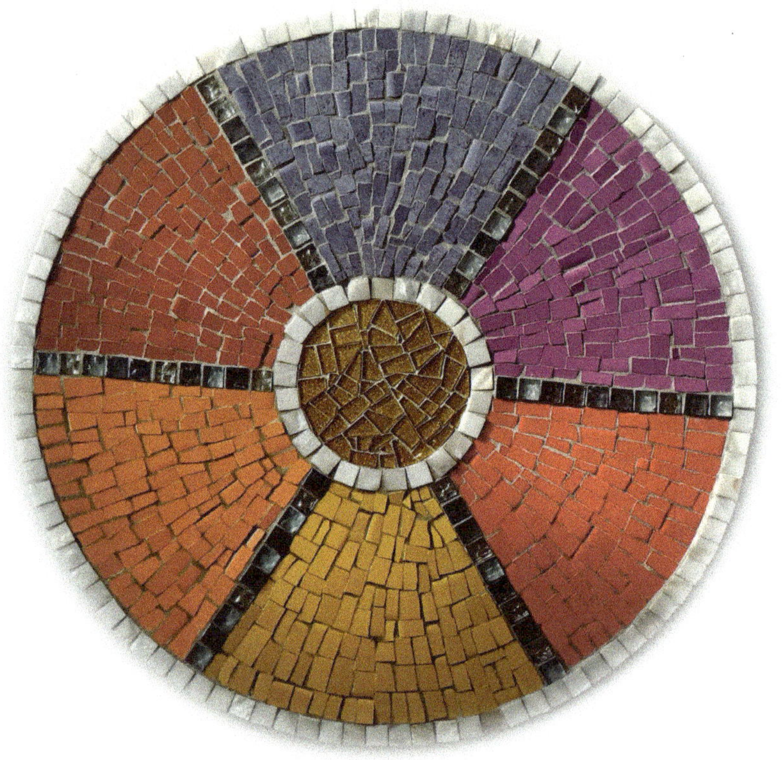

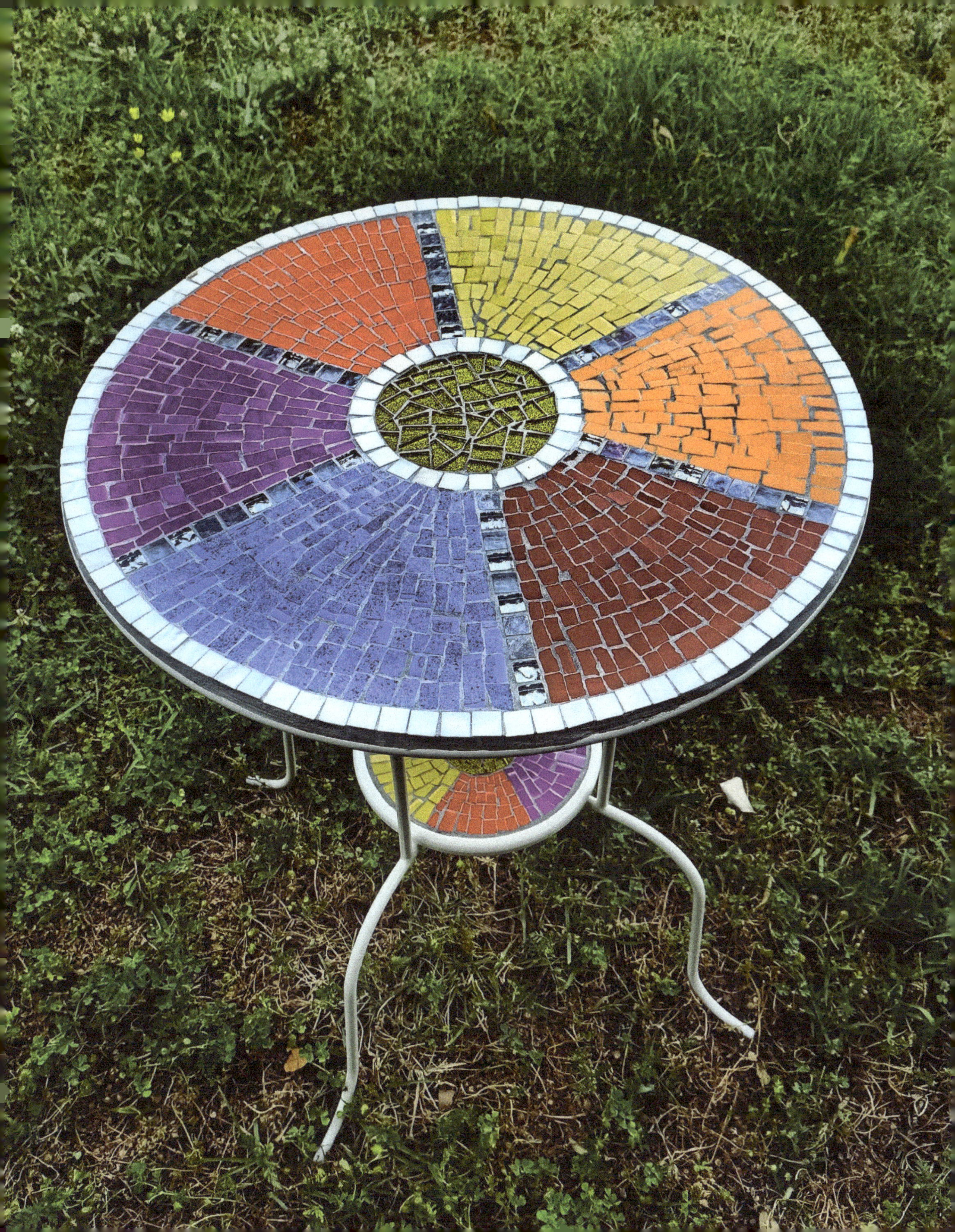

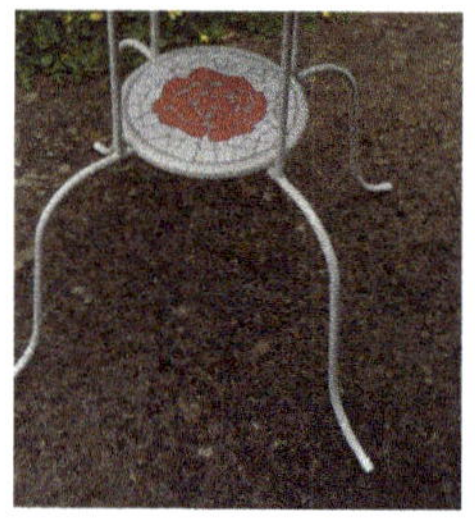

Project: A Rose Table

This rose table combines several techniques and ceramic tile cutting tools. The Work Process is taken from the stained-glass technique, where you cut each part separately that has a pre-defined shape. You need to have some patience in making this table since there are processes and stages that cannot be skipped: print out the rose and petals pattern, cut each part out of paper, copy it to the ceramics and cut each part precisely using the nippers. It's a great opportunity to learn how to use additional nippers, beyond the regular one. We'll learn why you should copy the pattern onto a ceramic cut into strips and how to use the parrot beak nipper. I guarantee you the result is worth the effort!

Materials:

A round metal table
Ceramics in shades of white, dark green, light green and red
Tile nipper
Parrot beak nipper (optional)
Combined nipper (optional)
Tie glue
Small glue bowl
A wooden stick or spatula
A thin screwdriver or toothpick
Light gray grout
Grout Gear: Mixing bowl, water, a wooden stick, rags, gloves

1 Print out the full table pattern. Trace in onto the table and number the parts.

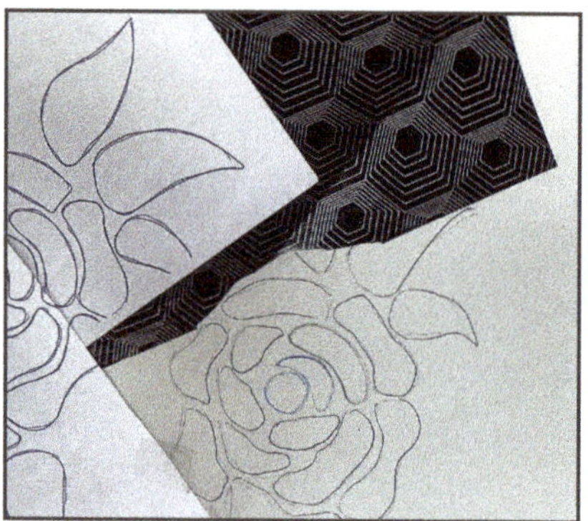

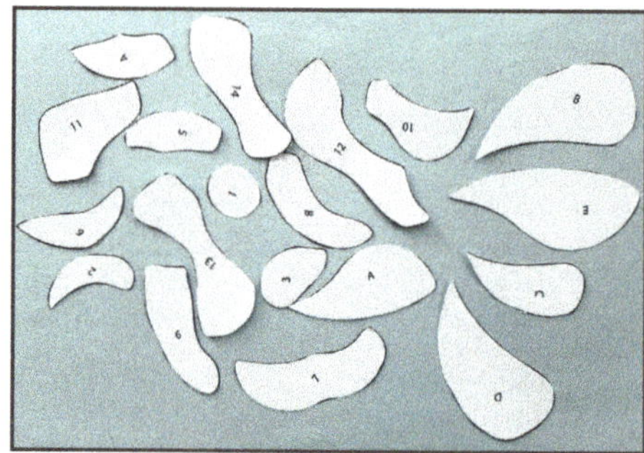

2 Print out one rose. Cut the numbered pieces, keep the red flower parts and the green leave parts separate.

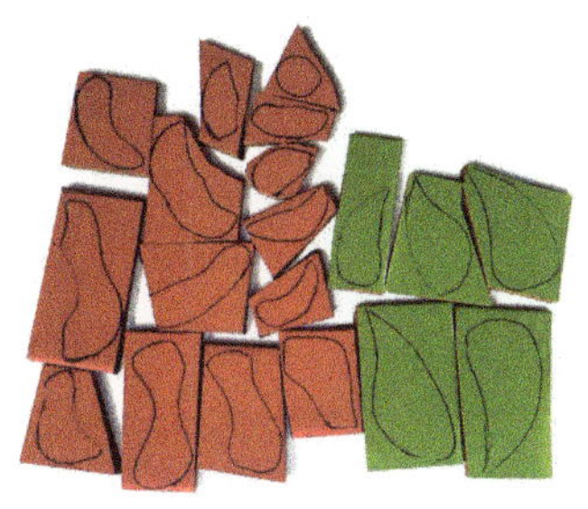

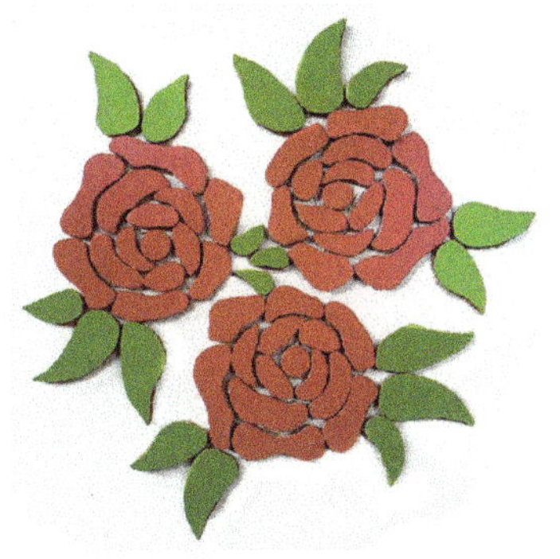

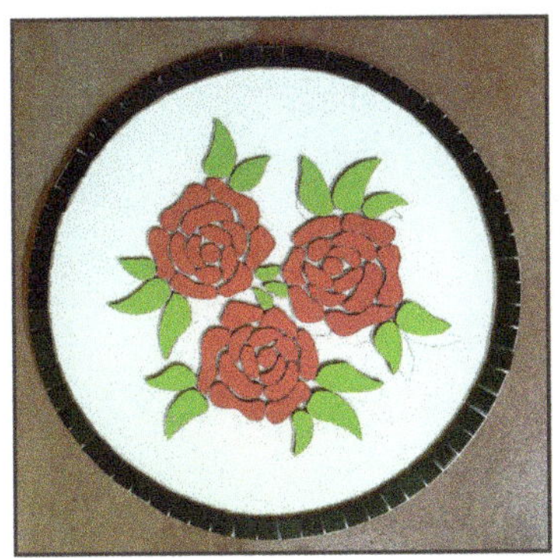

3 Copy the cut parts onto the ceramics using the right colored marker. See later on an explanation on how to cut the strips out of tiles that can make it easier. Number the pieces according to the paper. You should do it three times and keep the parts of each flower separate.

4 Cut the rose petals and green leaves (see how on pages 69-70) and glue each leave in its place, according to the numbering, using tile glue.

5 Glue dark green squares as the table frame. You can cut it with a cutting machine, combined nipper or use ready-made squares.

6 Fill the background with white ceramics, cut into random pieces.

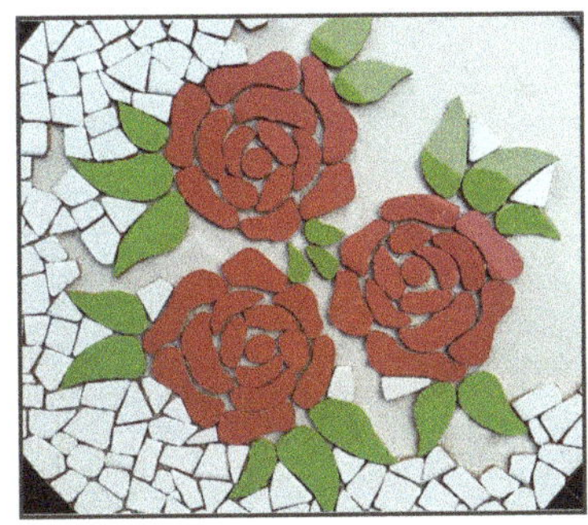

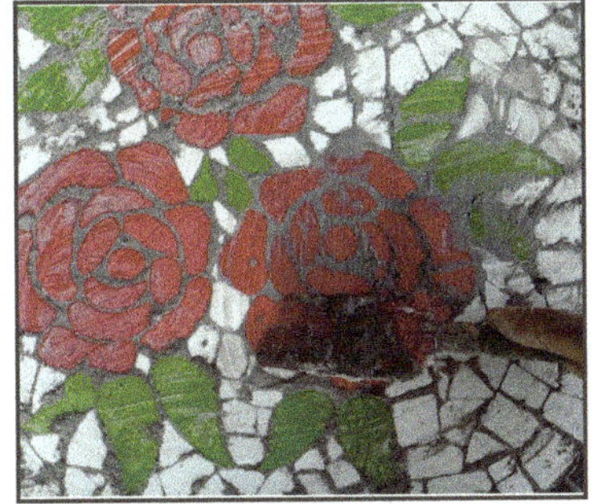

7 Wait for it to dry for a day and make gray grout, according to instructions. Clean and polish with rags and damp wipes. It's important to also have grout at the table frame, for a nice finish.

Pattern for the table:

Copy and enlarge according to the desire size.

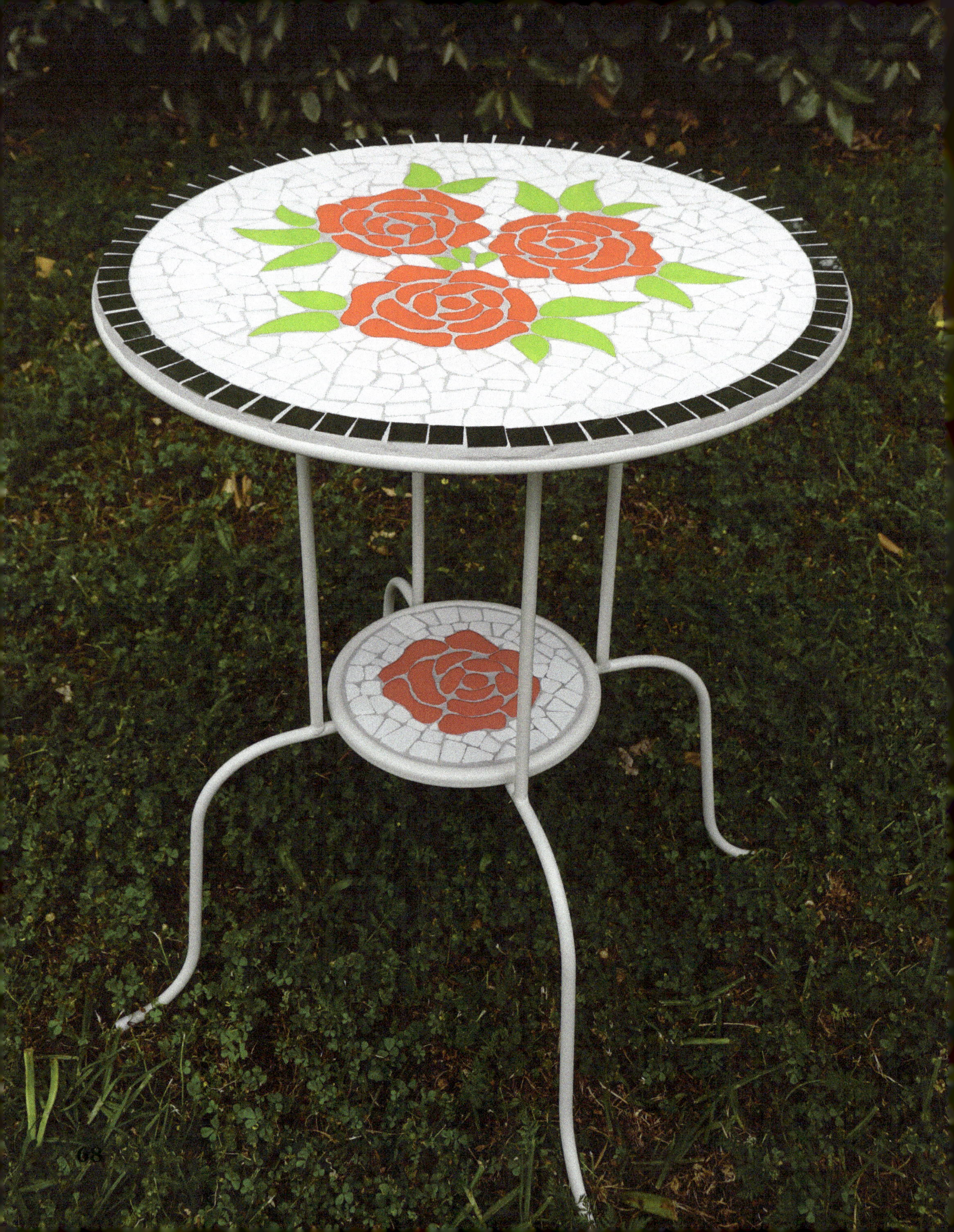

Cutting Strips Using a Combined Nipper

This device combines two devices used to cutting glass. A knife that scratches the tile and pliers that breaks in half. In case you've experienced in cutting glass, you already know the technique.

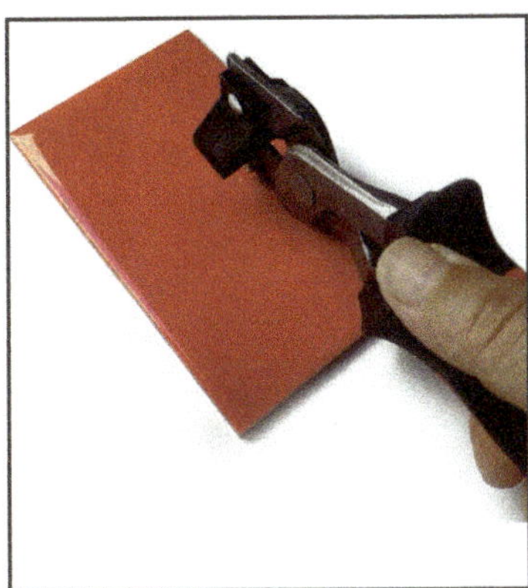

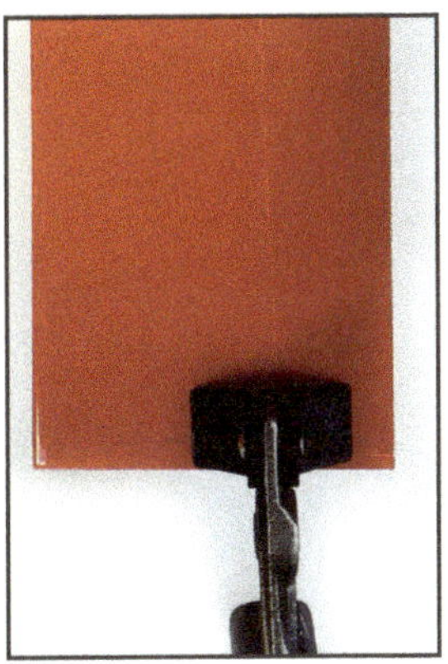

1 Place the wheeled nipper at the bottom of the tile and groove it from bottom to top. It's recommended to press the nipper and stabilize the hand to get a straight groove.

2 Place the tile between the two nipper parts, exactly at the center of the groove, and click.

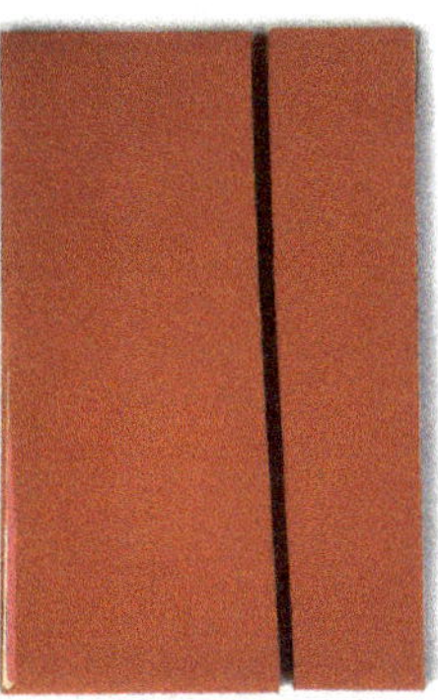

3 The tile will break in half along the entire groove.

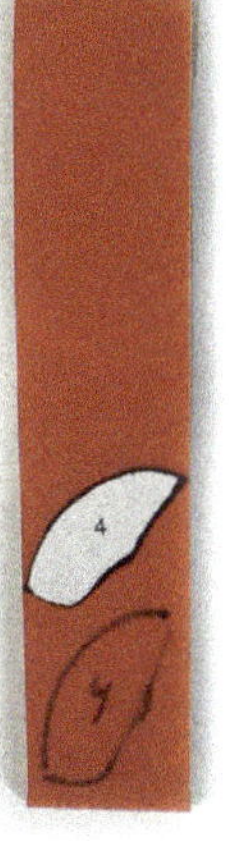

4 To make the rose table, you should cut a tile into strips. Place the cutout parts on the strip, copy a few parts onto one strip and separate them with the combined nipper. This way you'd make the best of the tile.

Cutting the Leaves

To cut the green leaves and the rose petals, use two nippers: ceramics nipper and parrot beak nipper. This will help cut curved spots.

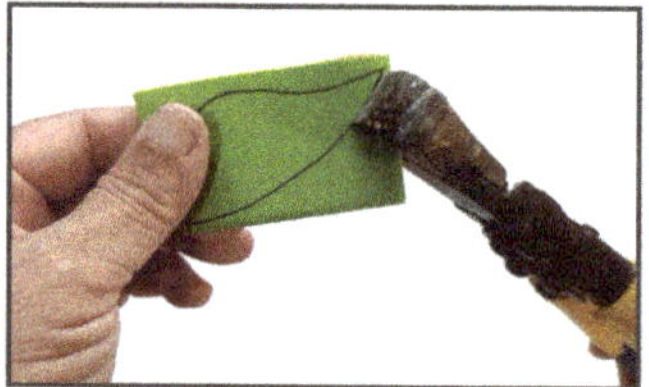

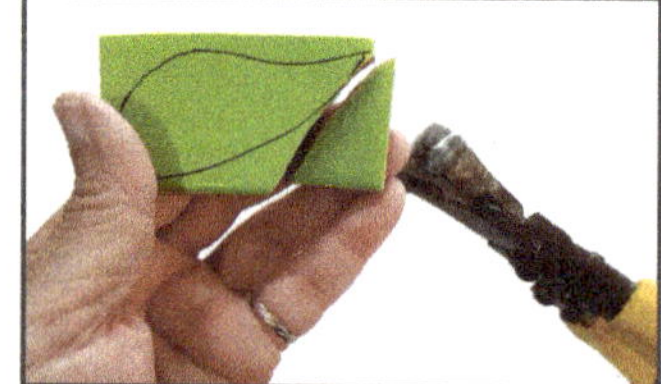

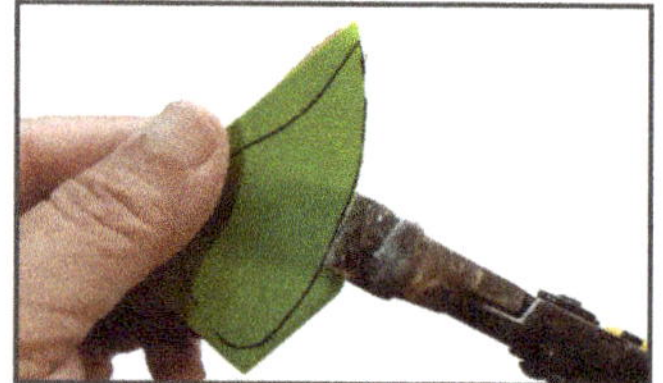

1 First, cut the wide brim around the sketched leave using the nipper.

2 Then, cut precisely along the line, slowly. Use the middle of the nipper, as of "biting" into the tile every time.

3 Cut the curved pieces with the parrot beak nipper – this nipper is used for creating a "enclave" in the tile. Complete and precise the leaf cutting using the nipper. In case you don't have a parrot beak nipper, you can use the regular nipper and cut slowly and gently, get into the enclaved part from the other side of the nipper each time.

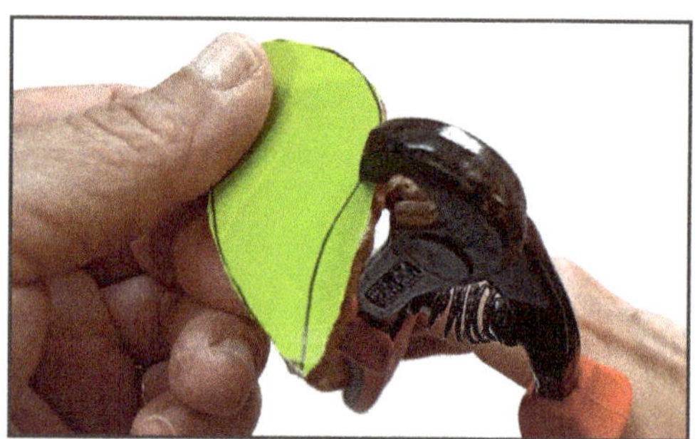

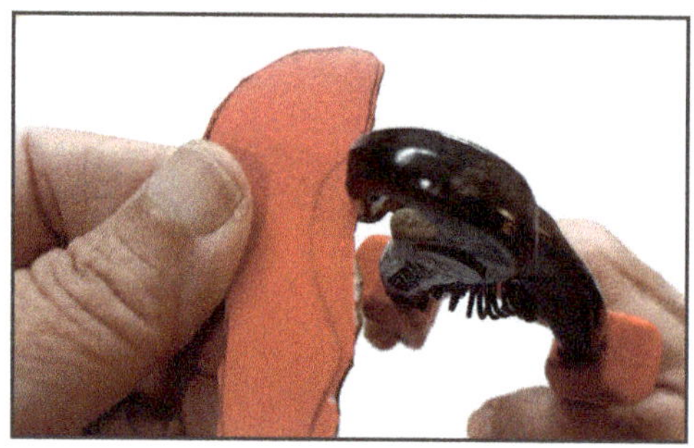

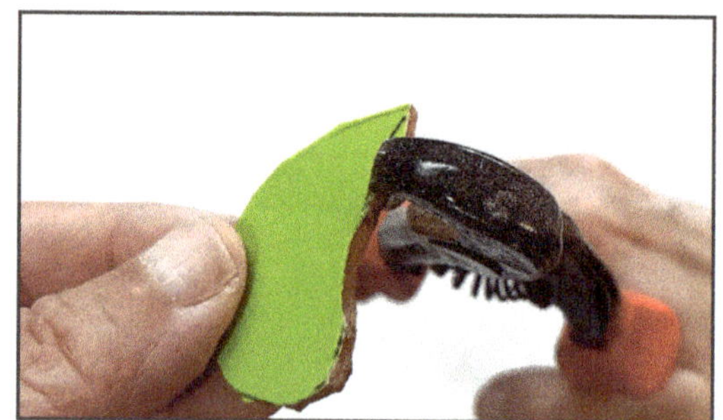

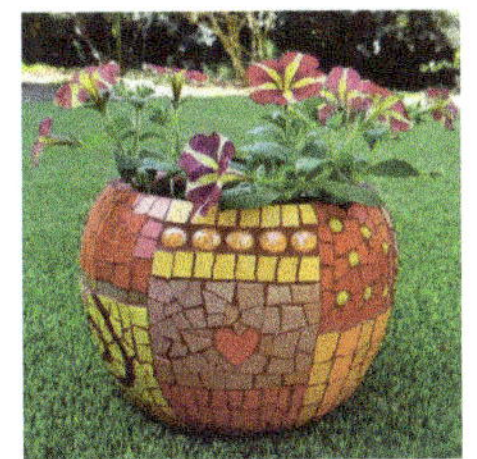

Project: Hearts Pot Plant

This pot plant started in a reverse – I wanted to fit it to a plant and took the color scheme from the colors of the flower. I chose two colors: red and yellow and added more shades in between. The pot plant pattern allows you to work with different types of materials and cutting shapes; each rectangle can be something else. Sometimes less is more… At the end, it's an opportunity to learn how to cut heart shapes from ceramic tiles.

Materials:

A round pot plant
Ceramic tiles in shades of red, yellow, orange, and pink.
Glass circles
Ceramic cutting nipper
Tie glue
Small glue bowl
A wooden stick or spatula
A thin screwdriver or toothpick
Brown grout
Grout Gear: Mixing bowl, water, a wooden stick, rags, gloves

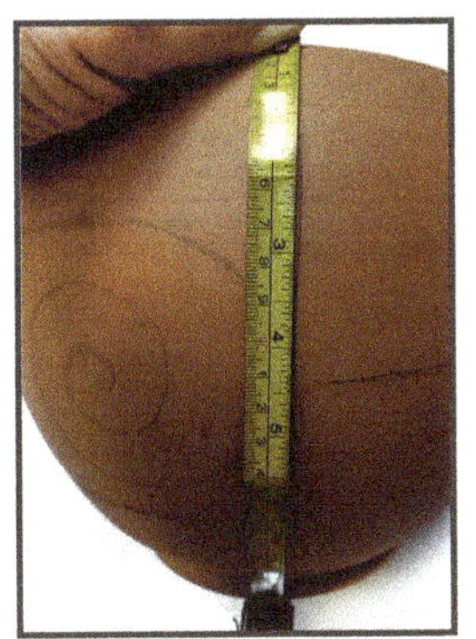

1 Trace the pattern onto the pot plant. You can use a flexible meter to mark the straight lines.

2 Cut heart shapes out of red ceramics and glue it in the middle of one of the parts (see explanation on page 72).

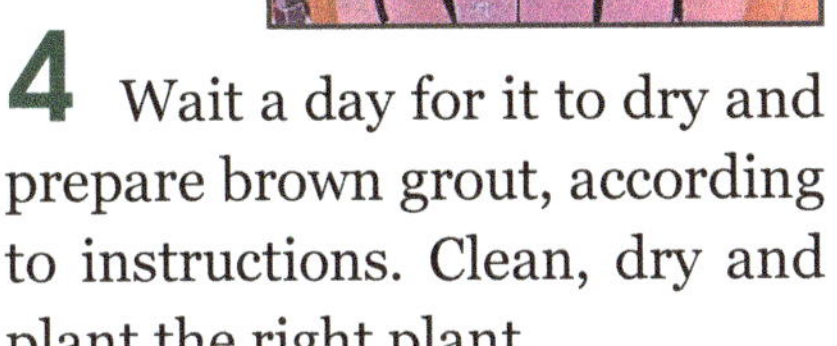

3 Cut the ceramics differently at each section: random pieces, short or long vertical lines, filling in a clean color or a mix and combination of glass circles. Combine the hearts within the rectangles.

4 Wait a day for it to dry and prepare brown grout, according to instructions. Clean, dry and plant the right plant.

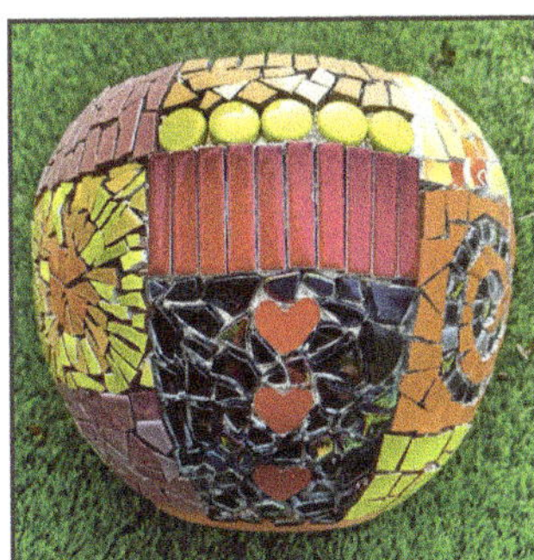
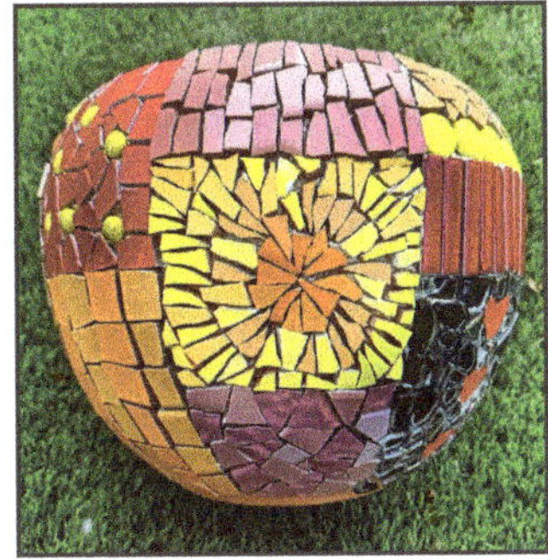
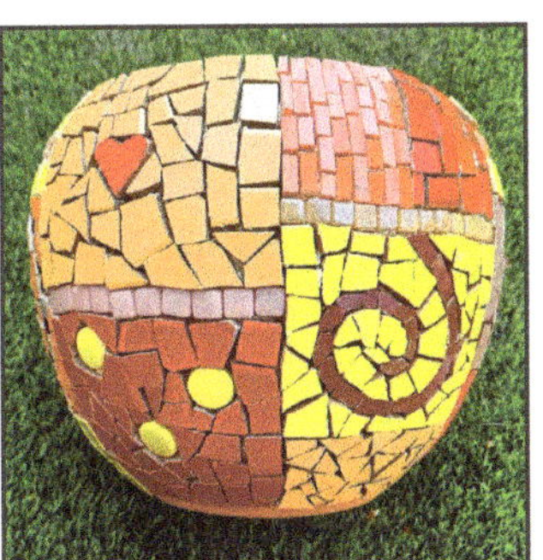
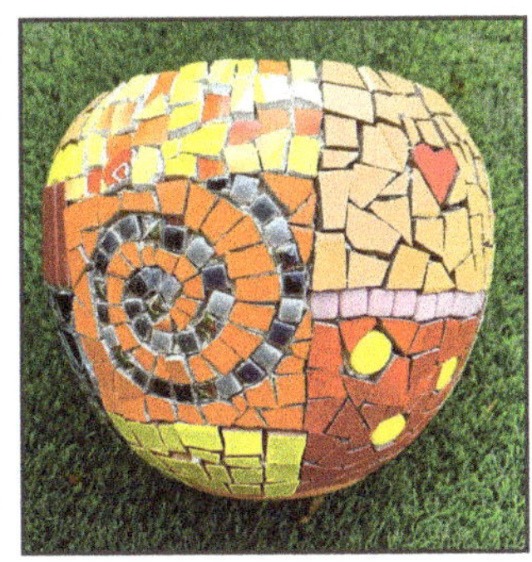

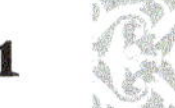

Cutting Ceramic Hearts

To cut the heart shape, we'll use two nippers: Ceramics nipper and parrot beak parrot, allowing us to "dig" into the ceramics and create the desired dent. Alternatively, you can also use a regular nipper and gently and slowly work to not break the shape.

1 Paint a heart on a cut tile using a marker.

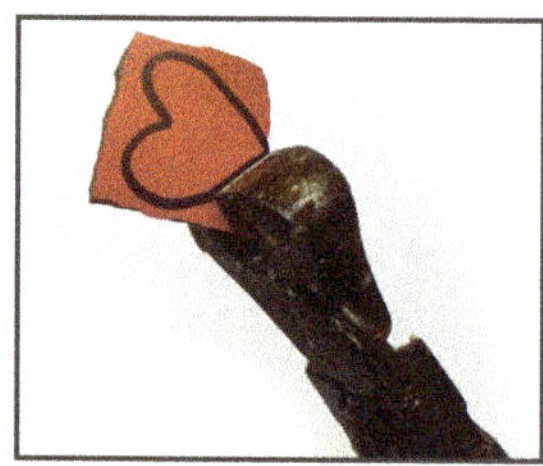

2 Start cutting the heart, from the bottom tip, using a tile cutting nipper.

3 Keep cutting along the line until the top.

4 Perform the same actions at the other side of the heart.

5 Straighten the cut as much as possible from the top, to get close to the painted image.

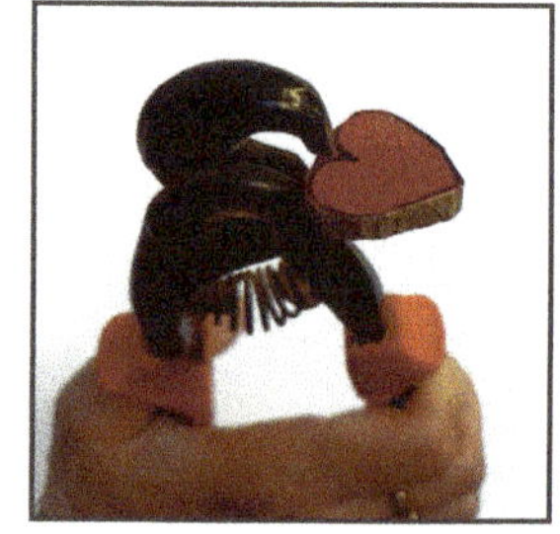

6 Using the parrot beak nipper, start to gently nibble the top center part of the heart.

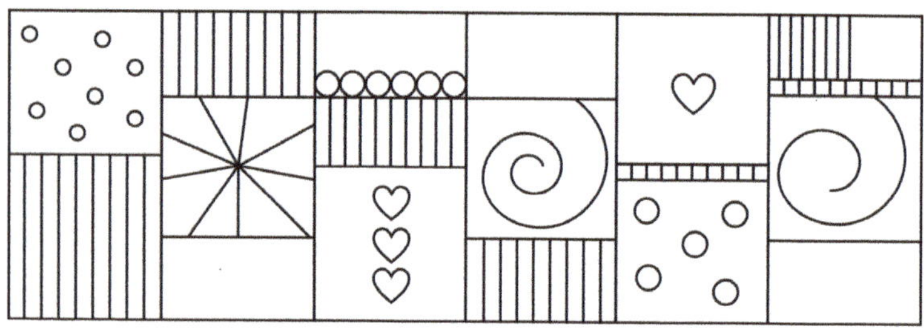

Pattern for the pot plant:
Copy and enlarge according to the desire size.

7 Cut along the line, one from right and once from left, very carefully. In case you don't have this nipper, you can complete the cut with the regular nipper, by cutting using the side of the nipper.

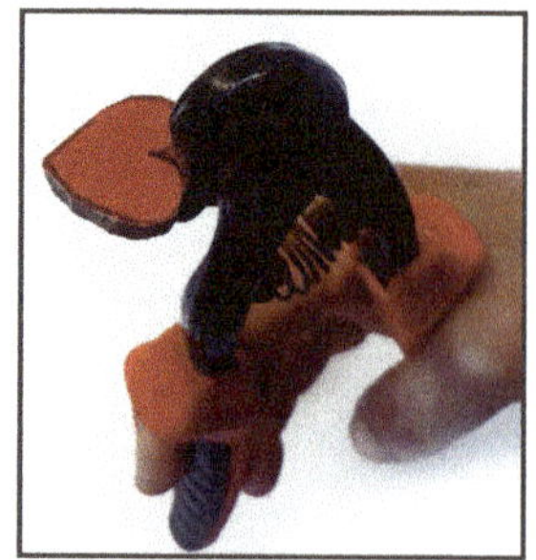

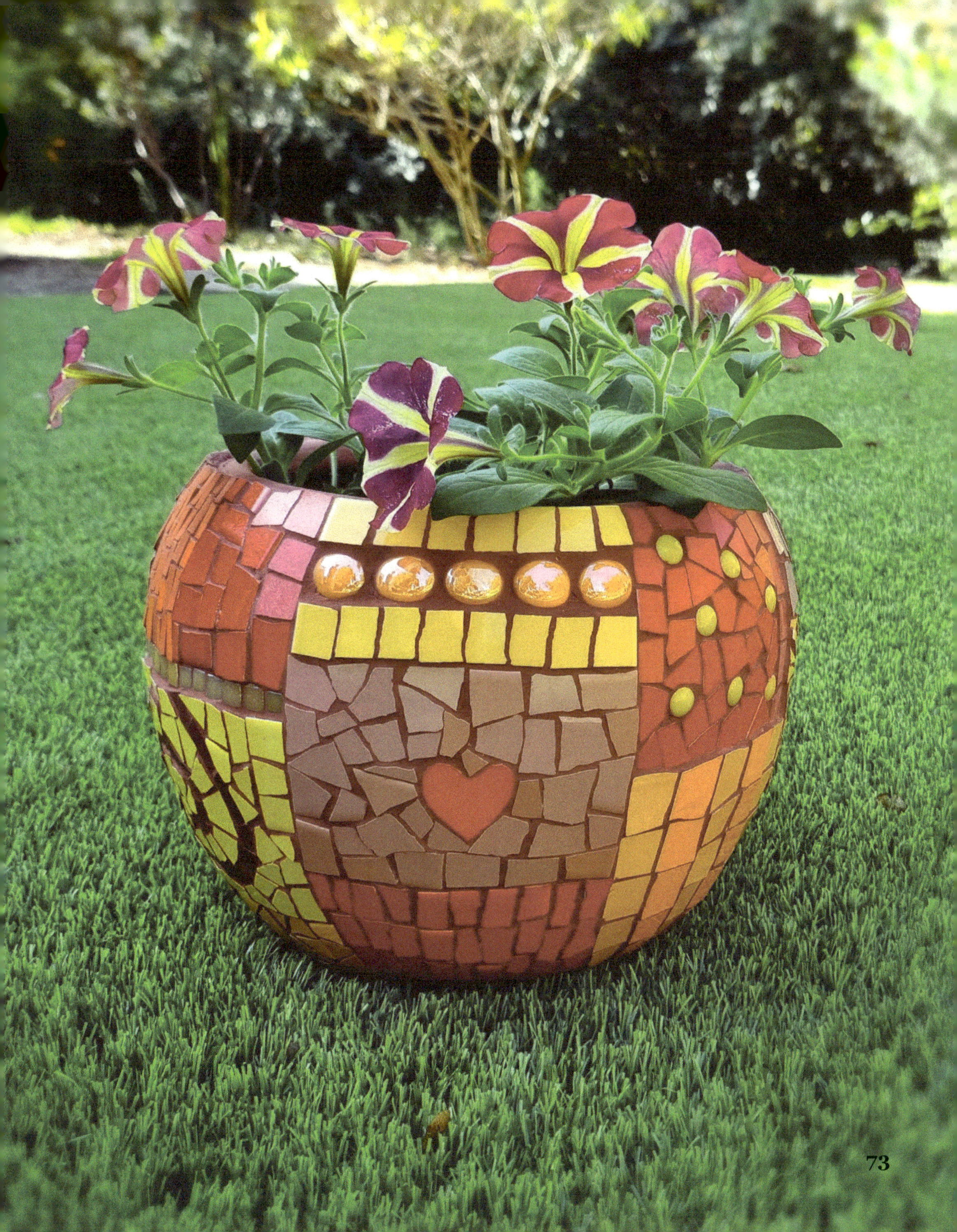

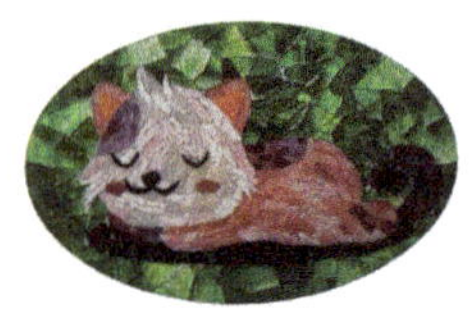

Project: Cat on Stone

At the front of my friend's house there is a rockery. I thought it would be nice to decorate it with colorful glass. Since it's hard to glue it directly onto the stone, there is a simpler and more accessible way. First, glue the mosaic onto a mesh and then cut and glue it onto the rock. This nice cat is the first of such "decorations" and I'm sure there will be more to follow.

The advantage of working with the mesh is its elasticity and the option of gluing on a surface that's not entirely straight. Working with glass allows us to create small and gentle shapes. The more shades of glass you will have, the richer it would look. This cute cat, of course, also can be glued on any wall you'd like.

Materials:

A fiberglass mesh cut into the desired sized rectangle
Cut up nylon, slightly bigger than the mesh
Stapler
Glass in shades of green, purple, and pink, some orange and black
A wheeled nipper
A brush
Tweezers
Plastic glue or carpenter's glue
Scissors
Small glue bowl
A wide spatula for applying glue
A thin screwdriver
Crème grout
Grout Gear: Mixing bowl, water a wooden stick, rags, gloves

Pattern for the cat:
Copy and enlarge according to the desire size.

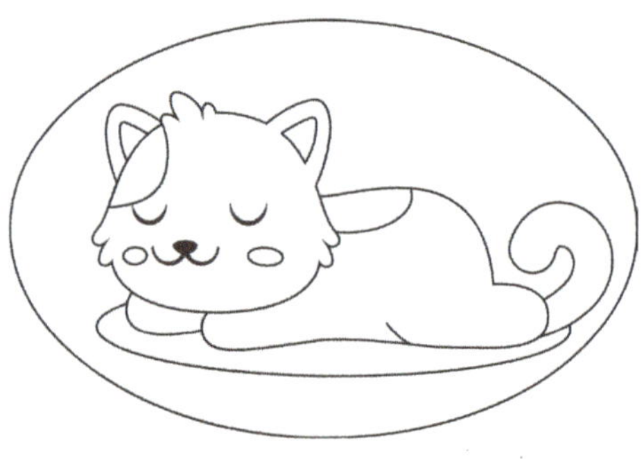

1 Print out the cat pattern, cut a mesh and nylon to fit. Staple the three pieces together in the following order: cat image, on to the nylon and a mesh on top of that.

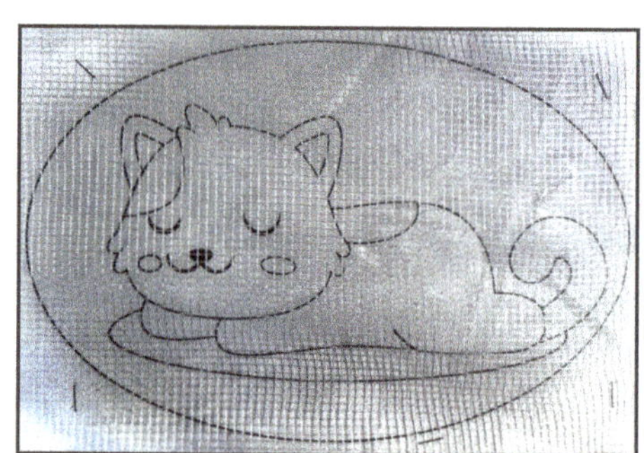

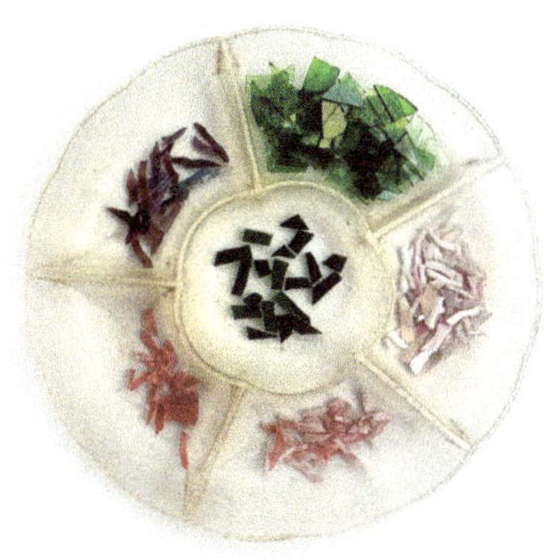

2 Prepare the cut glass in advance. It's recommended to use a partitioned plate; it will make it easier.

3 Using carpenter's glue (or a white plastic glue) glue on glass eyes and mouth from thinly cut glass, glued close together. An elliptical black stone can serve as the nose.

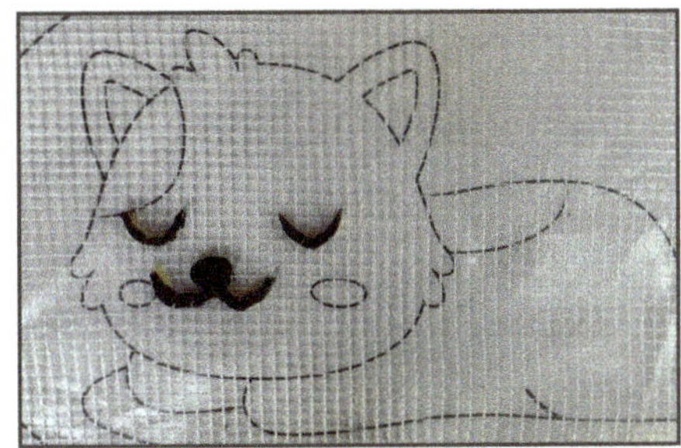

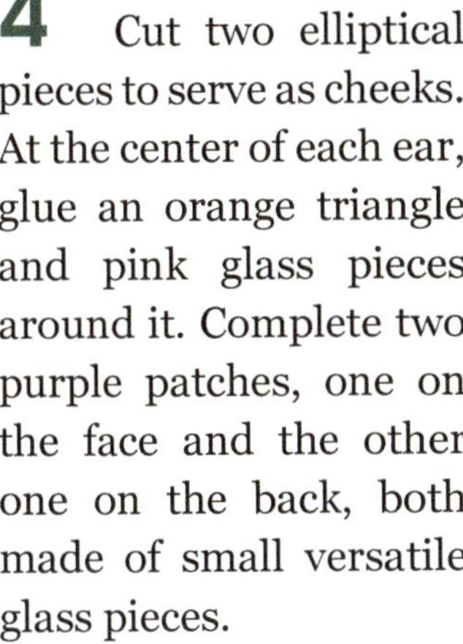

4 Cut two elliptical pieces to serve as cheeks. At the center of each ear, glue an orange triangle and pink glass pieces around it. Complete two purple patches, one on the face and the other one on the back, both made of small versatile glass pieces.

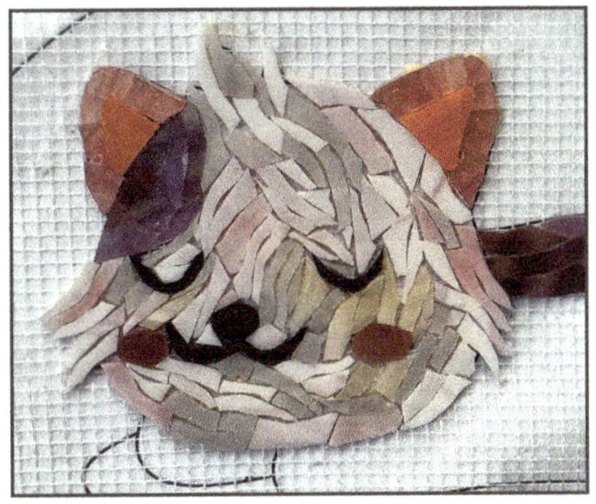

5 Using the wheeled nipper, cut long and thin strips of light pink shaded glass. Since the device has round wheels, they help create these kinds of pieces.

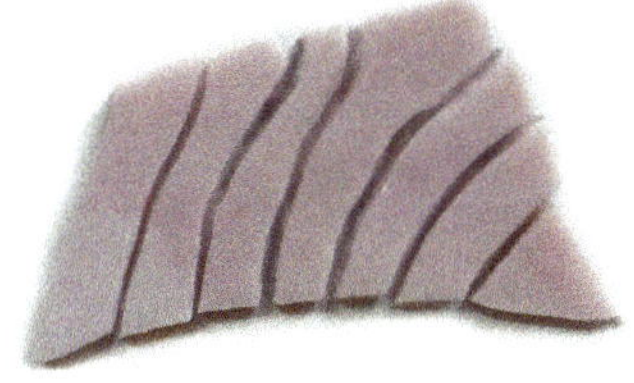

6 The body of the cat is also made of think stripes, this time in darker shades of pink.

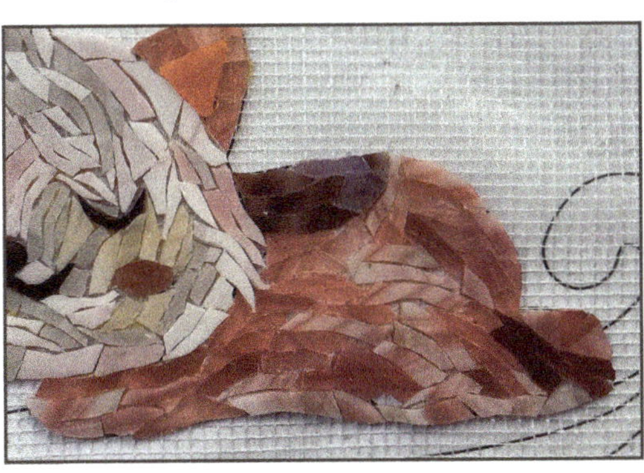

7 The cat's tail is made of small versatile purple glass pieces.

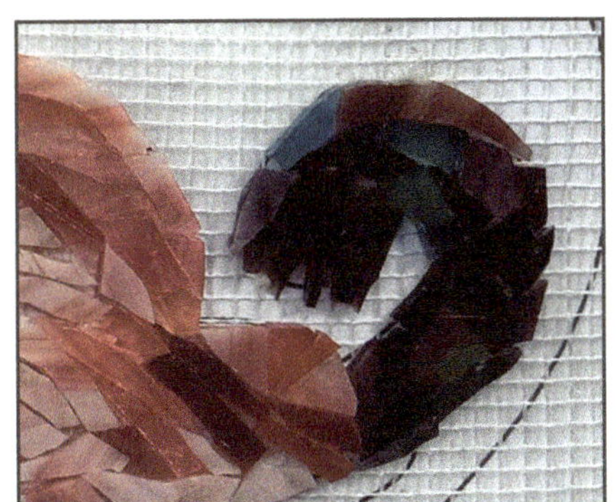

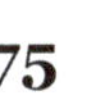

8 The cat is sitting on a rug, made of small glass pieces in dark green shades.

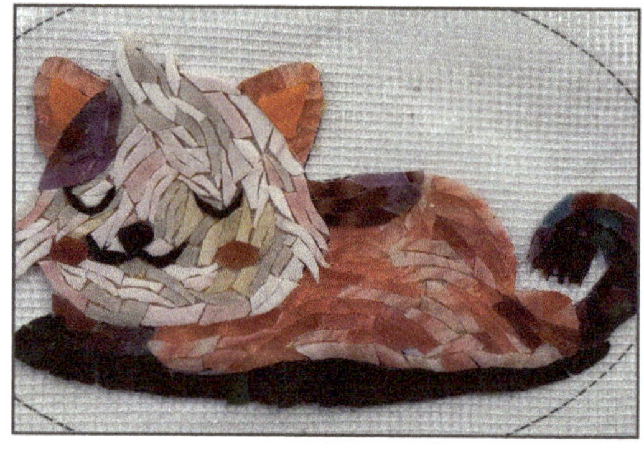

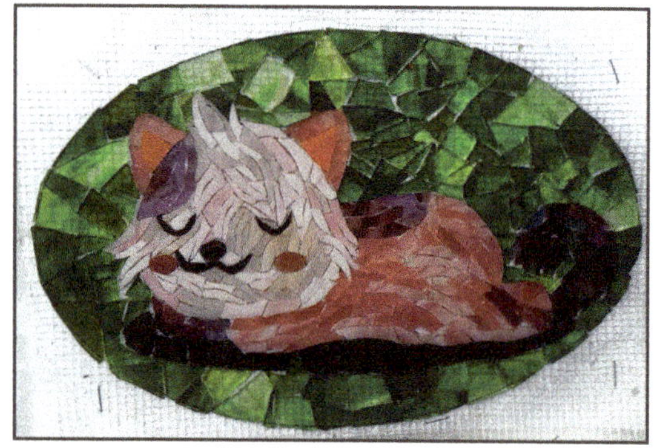

9 Complete the background using glass in various shades of green, cut into random pieces. It's important to make sure the edges are smoothy finished.

10 Wait a day or two for it to dry, separate the mesh from the nylon and cut as close to the mesh as possible.

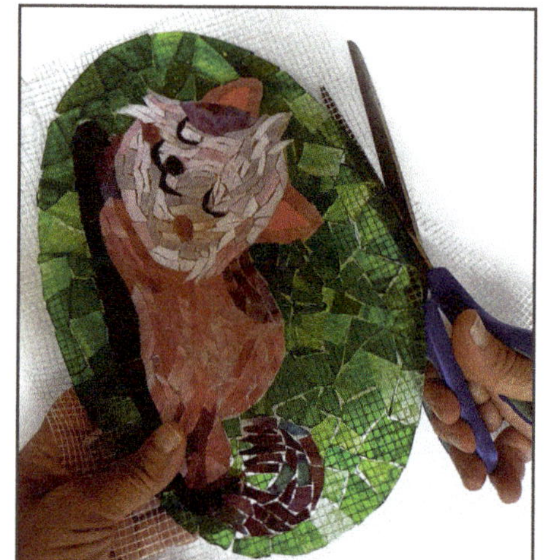

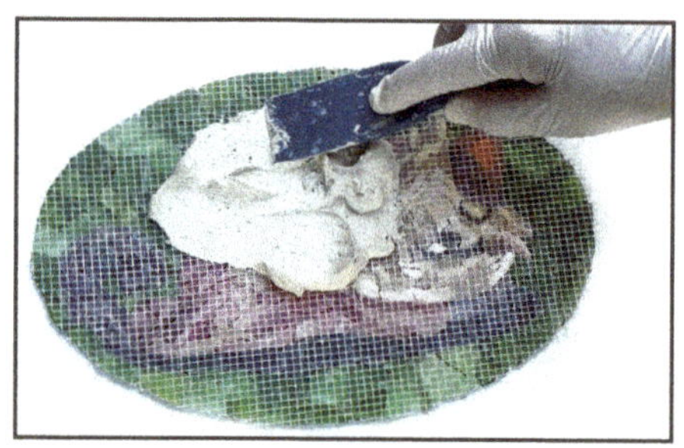

11 Using wide spatula, apply tile glue on the back of the piece. The amount of glue has to do with the how much the rock on which the mosaic is glued on would have to be smoothened.

12 Put the mosaic onto the stone and secure it tightly. You can gently hit it with your hands or use a wooden hammer, to make sure all the pieces are stuck. Take out the excess glue with a narrow screwdriver, before it all dries.

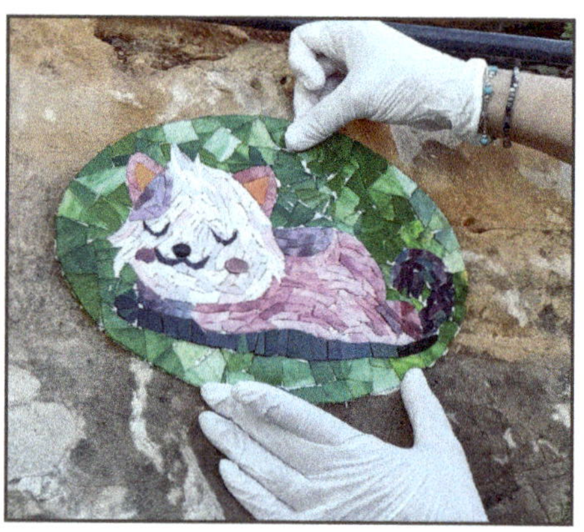

13 Wait at least 24 hours for it to dry and finish off with grout, directly onto the stone.

Tip: For gluing small pieces you can use tweezers – grab the glass using the tweezers and dip into the glue, without touching it with your hands.

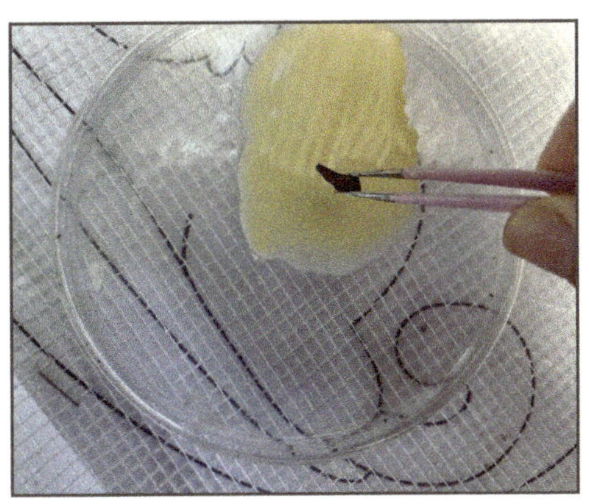

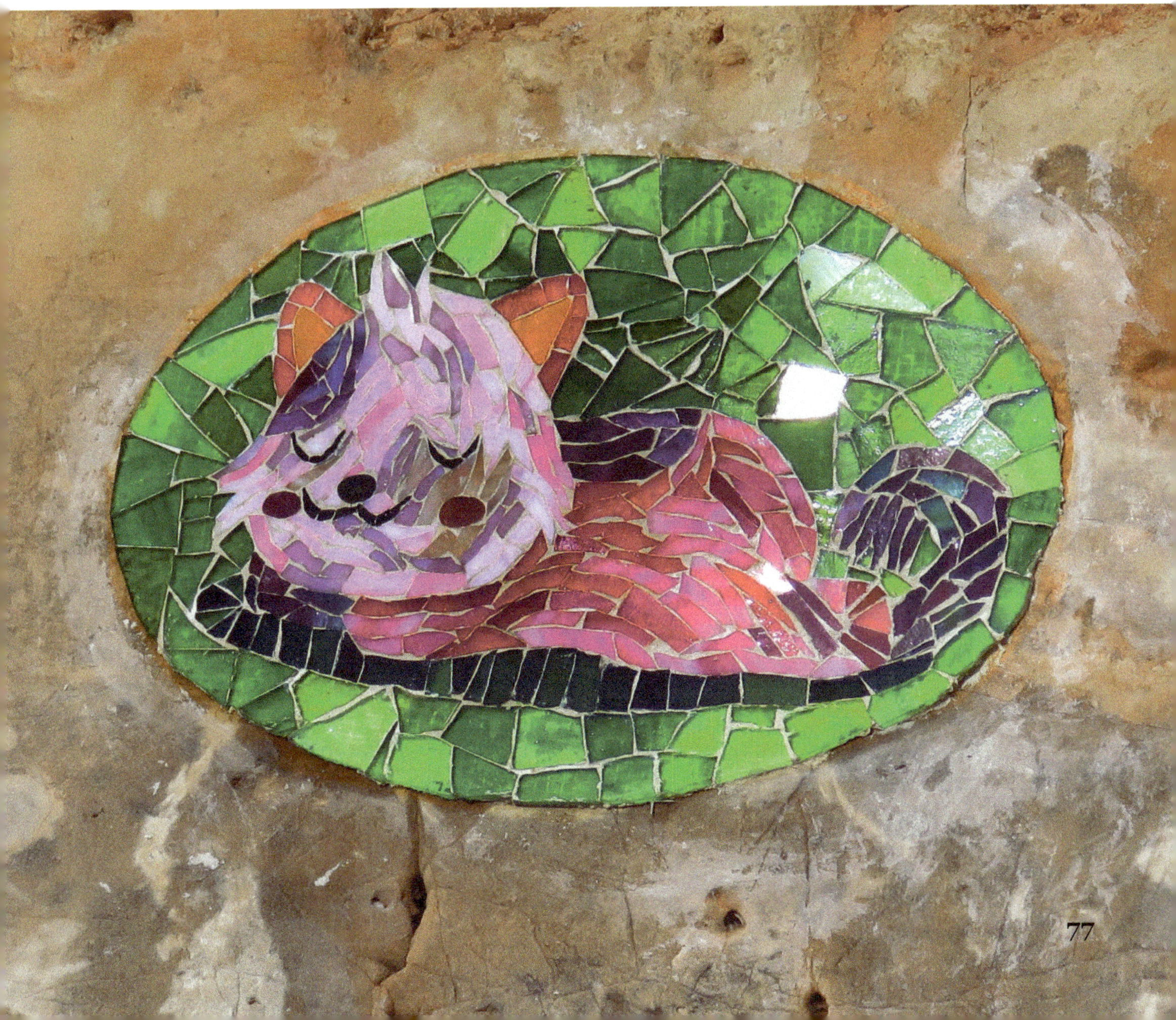

Project: Mosaic Covered Turtle

There are many 3-dimentional elements that can fit as a mosaic base, especially if they are made of stone or concrete – mushrooms, turtles, or other animals.

I received this turtle as a birthday present. I obviously couldn't leave it "naked", and he was given new life using plates, mirrors, ceramics, and glass shards. The result is very enjoying and if you make sure to work smoothly, you can even have children sit on it; they'd love to!

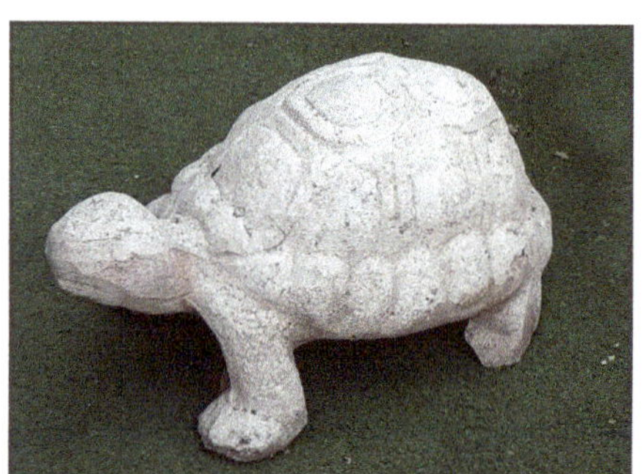

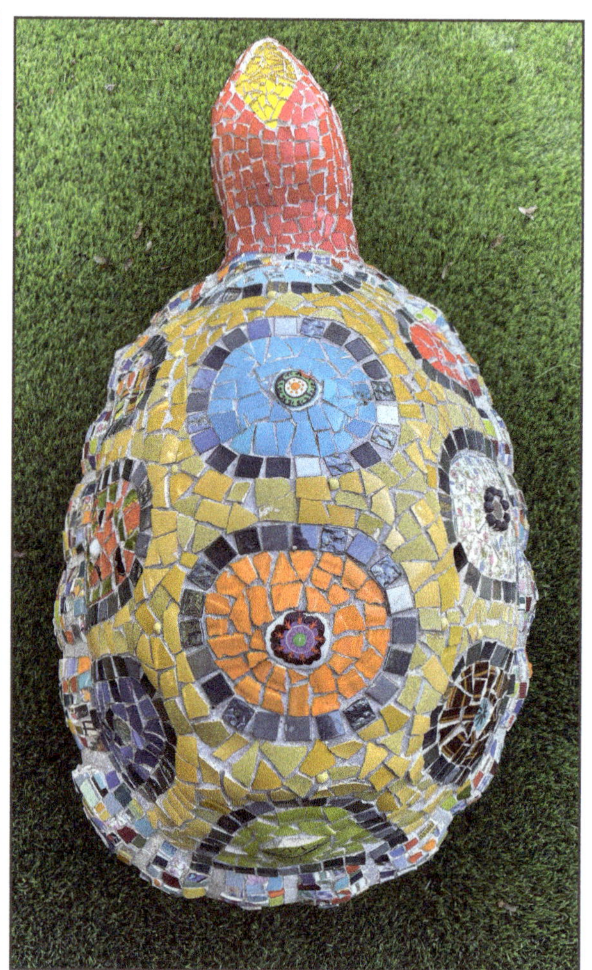

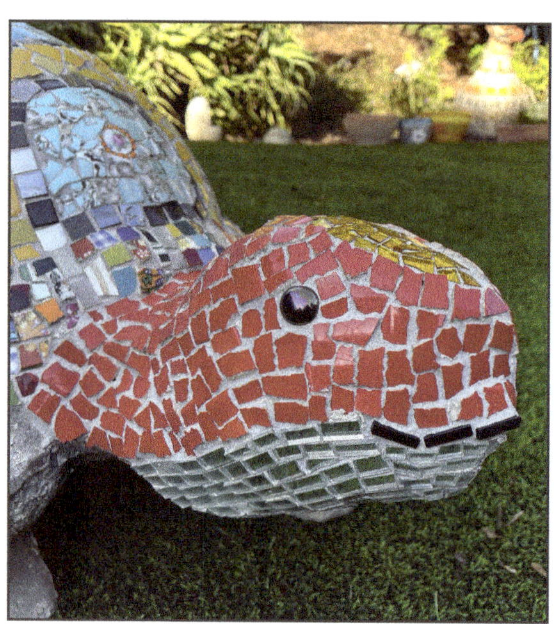

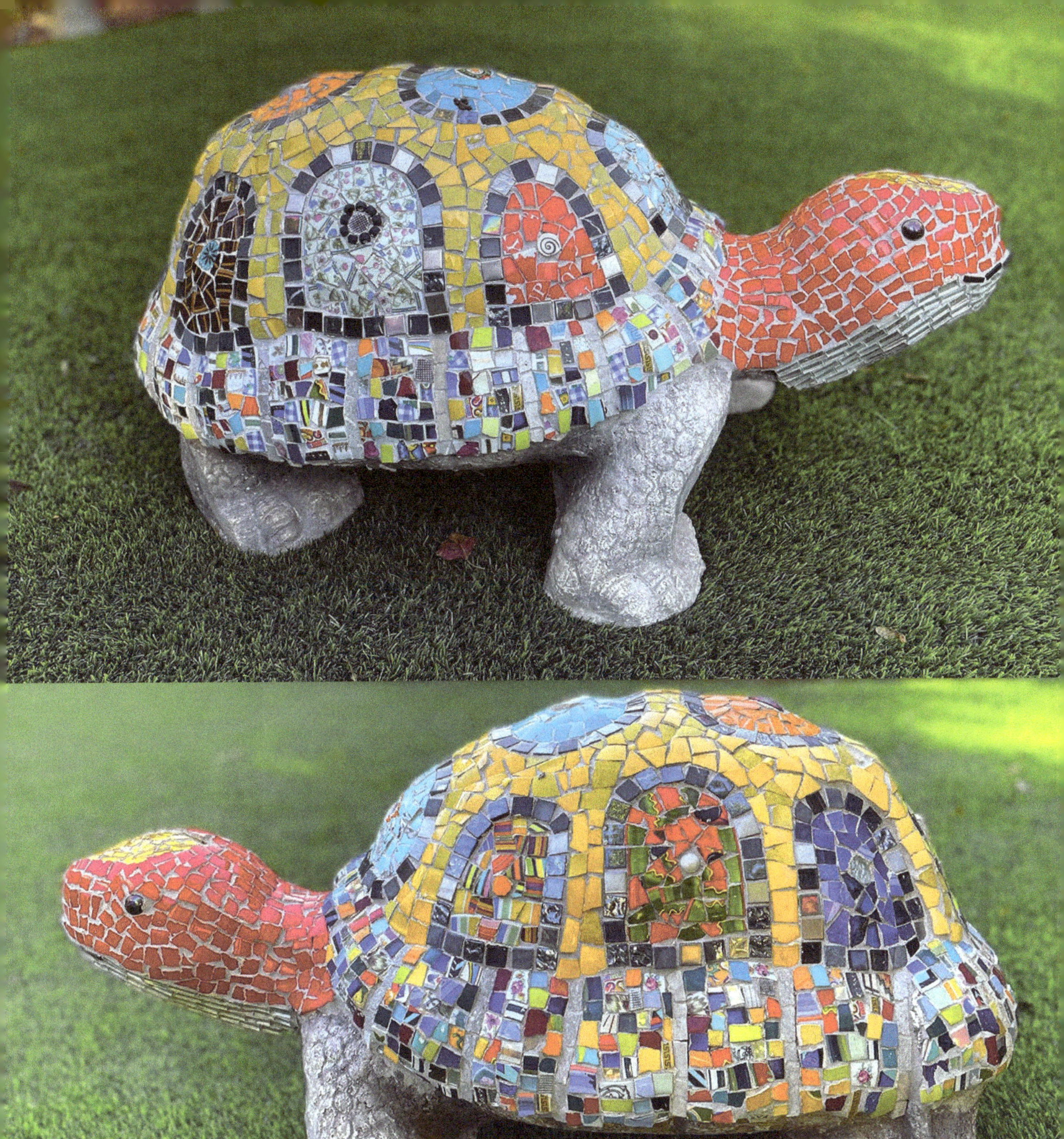

Summary

In this book, the ninth in the mosaic books for beginners, I've chosen to concentrate on projects that fit a garden. Maybe because I live in a house with a large garden decorated in colorful mosaic. I feel there are so many possibilities and I waned to share some of them using this book.

The range of options for the mosaic works is wide and there are always new things to learn. I'm always happy to find new materials, cutting methods or techniques I haven't heard of before. The mosaic makes all of those and more possible. I feel mosaicking is relaxing, gives peace and contributes to the joy of creating.

There were projects in the book that might fit a garden as well as ones that can be put indoors. We learned how to decorate trees, prepare a variety of pot plants, coat 2-dimensional or 3- dimensional elements. We were also exposed to the way in which recycling has great importance in the art of mosaic. now may be the time to ask your neighbors and friends not to throw away their cracked plates and cups, I'm sure you'd love to give them a "new life".

The book showed different cutting methods and inspected the difference between glass and ceramic cutting. They each use different tools as well as slightly different cutting technique.

We saw how a stunning mosaic table can be a refreshing and inspiring addition for hosting outdoors, and let's not forget to stress the importance of choosing the right base by which the table can last for many years.

The book presented several examples, but there's really no end to the mosaic work that can be created and it's important to learn the basics and then let your imagination run wild, come up with your own patterns or look of inspiration in different places.

I was glad to open a colorful hatch to the world of mosaic, which is a part of my life and that I love so much. My garden is already full of colorful mosaic pot plants, suspended spheres, turtles, and tables.

Even if you don't have a garden, I'm sure you'll find a place for at least one colorful pot plant of your doing. It's not complicated, it sometimes takes time, but one thing's for sure – it's all worth it!

Keep it creative,

Yours,

Sigalit Eshet

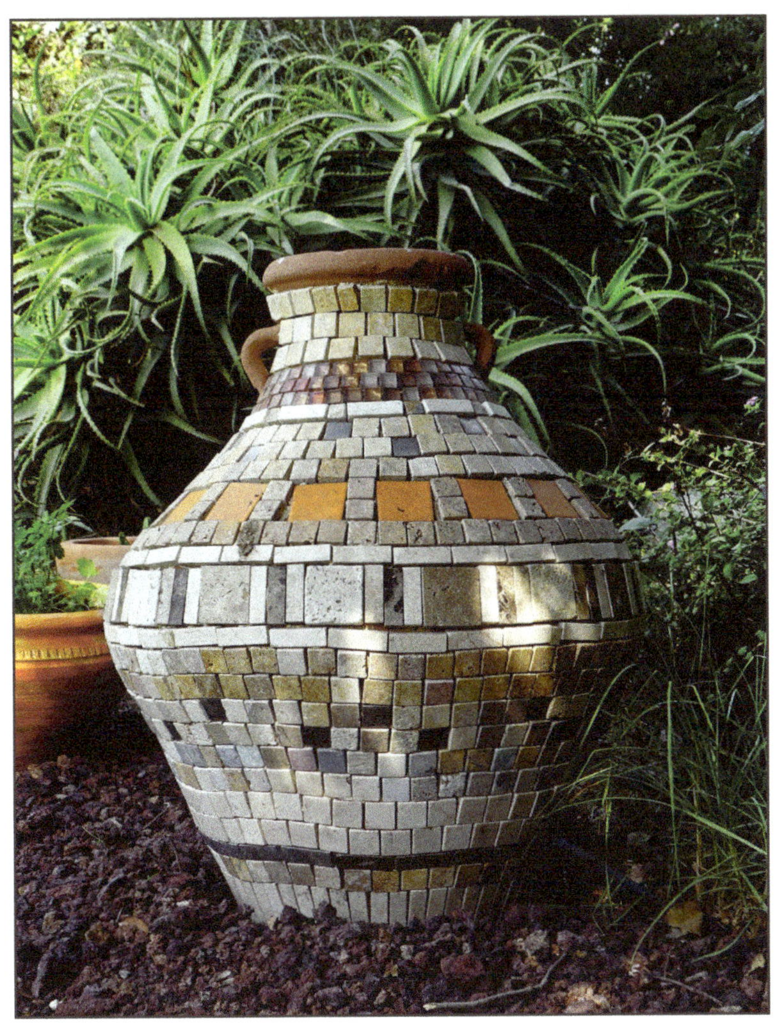

Other mosaic books on Amazon:

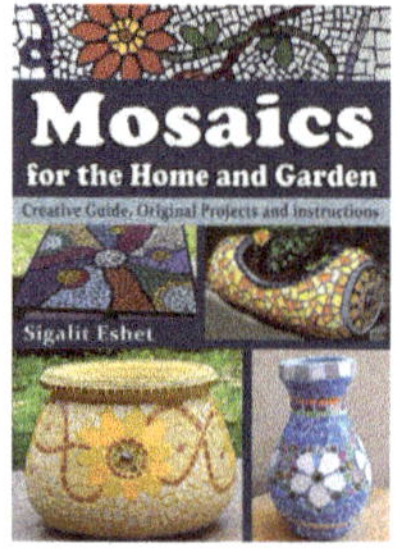

Mosaics for the Home and Garden

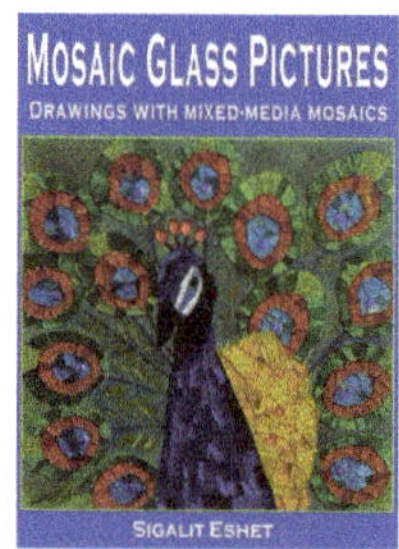

Mosaic Glass Pictures

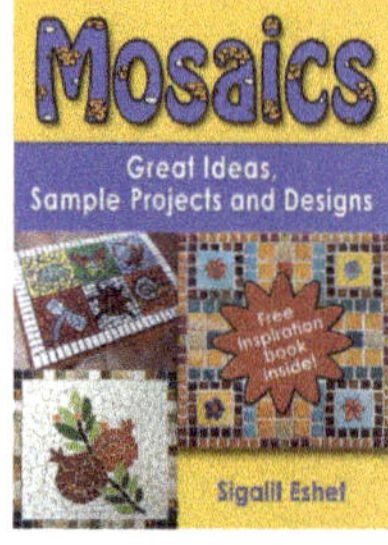

Mosaics: Great Ideas and Projects

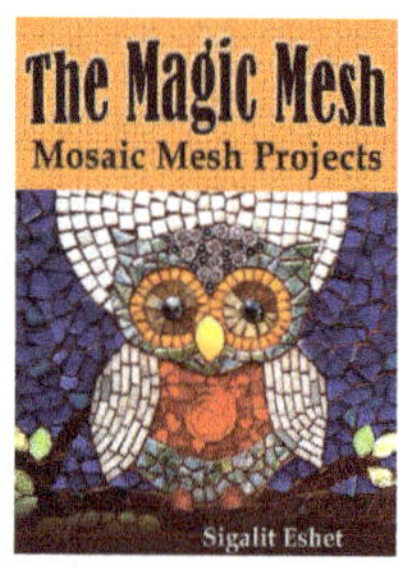

The Magic Mesh: Mosaic Mesh Projects

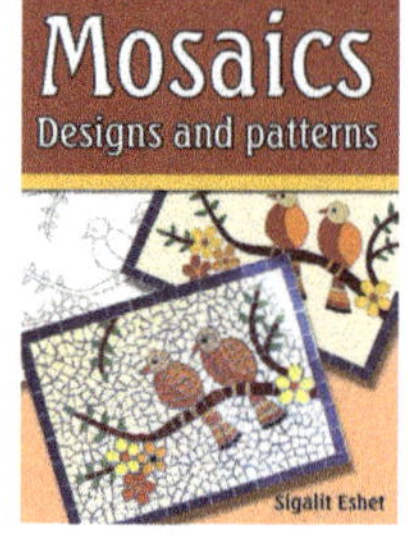

Mosaics - Designs and patterns

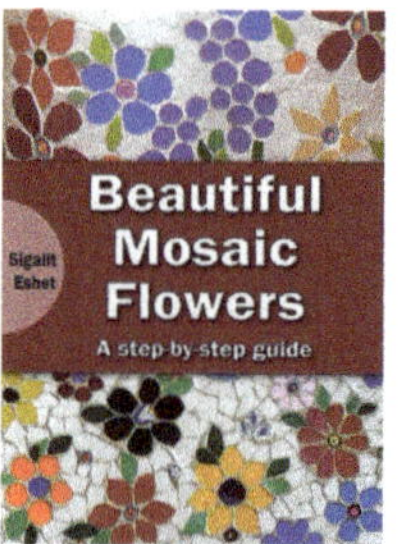

Beautiful Mosaic Flowers

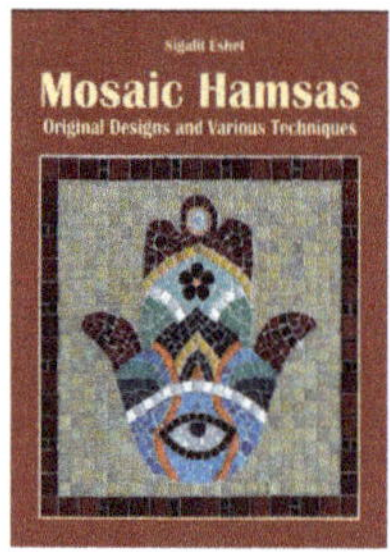

Mosaic Hamsas: Original Designs and Various Techniques

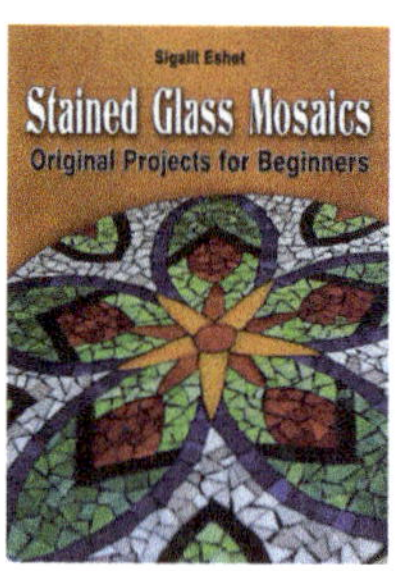

Stained Glass Mosaic

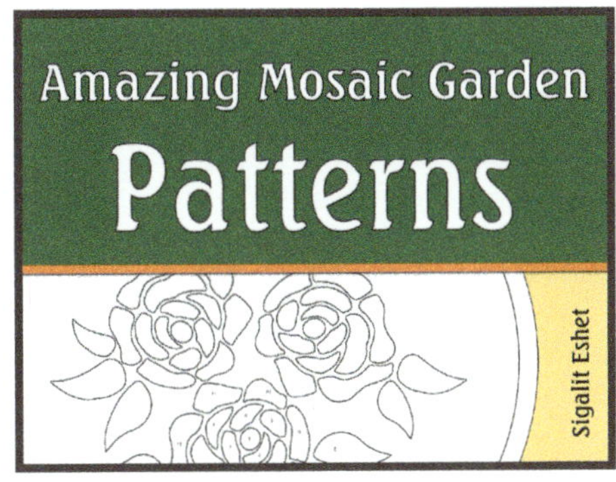

There is a bonus for you. All the patterns that are showed in this book, are available in a pdf file, for your use:
Just type **https://bit.ly/3GpY8Jv** in your browser and get it or scan the QR.

If from some reason you can't get the file, please email me and I will mail it to you: **sigalit@sigalit.art**

If you loved this book, **Please leave a review on Amazon** and let other people enjoy making a great mosaic garden.

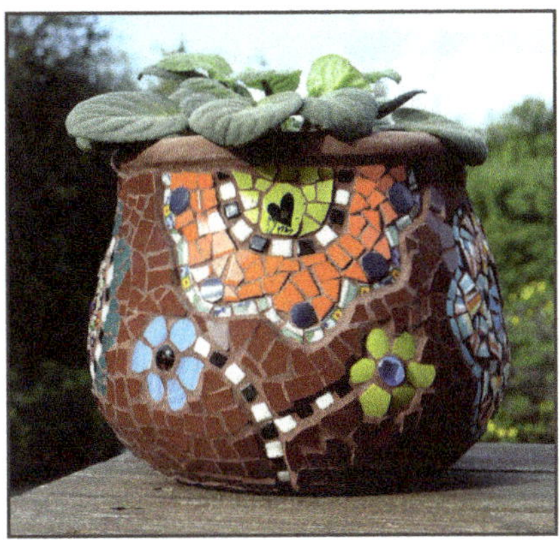

Sigalit@sigalit.art

www.sigalit.art

f **SigalitBooks**

etsy **Sigalitarts**

a **amazon.com/author/sigaliteshet**

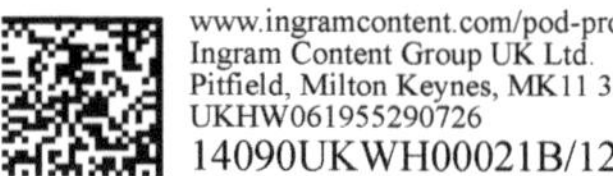

www.ingramcontent.com/pod-product-compliance
Ingram Content Group UK Ltd.
Pitfield, Milton Keynes, MK11 3LW, UK
UKHW061955290726
14090UKWH00021B/1242

9 789659 282760